Rock Solid

Football, Family, Faith, and Friends

Rocky Calmus
with Linda Calmus

insight publishing group
Tulsa, Oklahoma

ROCK SOLID

Rock Solid by Rocky Calmus with Linda Calmus
Published by Insight Publishing Group
8801 S. Yale, Suite 410
Tulsa, OK 74137
918-493-1718

Cover photographs and football action shots by Mary Engles unless otherwise noted.

1st Printing

ISBN-1-890900-43-5
Library of Congress catalog card number: 2002103929
Printed in the United States of America

For additional copies contact:

Straight From the Heart
Bill Horn
Phone: (405) 396-0200
Fax: (405) 396-0300

Table of Contents

DEDICATION

Rocky, this book is about you, the baby of our family. I realize that you are somewhat embarrassed and are convinced you live a boring life, but I assure you that's not the case. People want to know about athletes and heroes, and you are one!

Myrle and I were blessed with not one but *four* beautiful, talented children—Lance, Richie, Mandy, and Rocky. The Calmus and Ayres families are two stellar heritages that demonstrate love, devotion, and hardworking values, and the Lord has been so very giving to us throughout our lives. He has blessed Rocky abundantly with extraordinary skills and perseverance, making this book possible.

Family, friends, neighbors, church, loved ones, teachers, coaches, Oklahoma University, and fans—thank you all for this opportunity to share our story, the story of "Rock Solid."

Love Always,
Your Mama
(Linda Calmus)

ACKNOWLEDGEMENTS

Rocky, thanks for all the fun, excitement, and recognition you have provided us through your endeavors. You have persevered, worked hard (and studied harder), and we've enjoyed the ride.

Thanks to my best friend, photographer, typist, computer expert, and great listener. Your encouragement, prayers, faith, and cheerleading have been a driving force in this book. Mary, you and Rob are our best friends. You have been so supportive; we love you and your family—Nathan, Dillon, and Crystal Engles—and special thanks to your sister, Linda Warner, for giving us the idea to write this book.

Thanks to John Mason and his staff at Insight Publishing Group for accepting this manuscript and making it readable and helping it flow better.

Thanks to Bill Horn, Rocky's marketing agent, for his encouraging faith and perseverance for this book.

Linda Calmus

Mary Engles and Linda Calmus

FOREWORD

by Head Coach for
Univerisity of Oklahoma, Bob Stoops

Some play a position in football; others define the position they play. During his time at OU, Rocky Calmus was the consummate linebacker, and he was also the consummate Sooner.

I had the good fortune of coaching Rocky for three and a half years, and during that time, he impressed me in many ways—most of which were behind the scenes and never witnessed by the public.

Rocky was a businesslike worker who took pride in doing everything to its fullest. He never rounded a corner or took a shortcut. When he realized that he needed to put on size, he worked on both size and speed through great effort in the weight room and through running exercises, and the other players in the program knew of Rocky's high expectations for himself. It raised the bar for the whole team. But Rocky's good example went far beyond training habits; his toughness and determination was truly unique.

Rocky is the only individual I've ever seen return to the field just *one week* after breaking his leg. He also played through OU's whole National Championship winning season with a cast on his hand from a broken wrist, and he still managed to lead the team in tackles for the year.

Rocky was a two-year captain and a four-year starter. He helped us to a record of 24-2 for the 2000 and 2001 seasons, and, of course, he was a centerpiece on the 2000 team that won a Big XII and National Championship and went 13-0. Rocky left OU as the fourth leading tackler in Oklahoma University history, an impressive achievement considering the many great players that have come through OU. He also won the Butkus Award as the nation's top linebacker.

Good things happen to good people

Rocky won so much acclaim because he was a great Sooner football player; he was a great Sooner football player because of his exceptional quality as a human being. I enjoyed coaching Rocky as much as any coach can enjoy a player, but I have enjoyed knowing him and counting him among my friends much more so.

INTRODUCTION

by University of Oklahoma Co-Defensive Coordinator/Linebacker Coach, Brent Venables

Rocky Calmus is a very rich young man. Rocky is one of the "richest" people I have ever met. However, I'm not referring to that in the monetary sense, for even as this book is being published, Rocky has not even signed an NFL contract. Rocky has achieved status as an elite football player on the field. He has been recognized with virtually every honor a collegiate football player can receive—from All-League, to Big XII Defensive Player of the Year, to OU's Defensive MVP, to All-American, to team captain, to winning the coveted Butkus Award as the nation's finest linebacker. That my friend, is one heck of a hardware collection.

Over the past three years, Rocky has made nearly every play he was meant to make. His instincts, toughness, and desire make him the great player he is. Rocky is, without question, the most competitive player I've been around. He desires to be a superior player and is willing to do *whatever* it takes to get it done. If you serve Rocky Calmus with a challenge, he'll decimate it with the fury of an atomic bomb.

It is also important to mention that Rocky and many of his teammates chose to come to Oklahoma University during some very lean years when it was very unpopular to do so. They did not feel threatened by the challenge that lay ahead. They, in fact, relished the opportunity to awake a sleeping giant. And they did, earning a Big XII Conference Championship, a National Championship, and a 31-7 record in the last three years. The excitement is back, the swagger is back, and the excellence and the University of Oklahoma are back! In the minds of many, Rocky Calmus is the poster boy for the resurrection of OU football.

However, Rocky should not be defined only by his accomplishments on the field. In my mind, Rocky is defined by that for which he stands. Rocky is made from a mold that *all men*, athletes or not, should follow, and he represents what *is* right with today's society. Rocky possesses impeccable character. He has continually embraced a leadership role in the extremely difficult, challenging, and ever-changing society with which our young people deal. He is defined by the admirable relationship he has with his family and close friends. The support and love given by his family is almost numbing. Rocky is defined by his humility, morality, and the values he holds dear. He has a strong belief in his faith and the good Lord. Believe me, he practices what he preaches, and he epitomizes the phrase "say what you mean, and mean what you say." Rocky has set the bar pretty high in the past three years. He has led by his actions, by his commitment, and by his pursuit of excellence both on and off the field.

I know Rocky dreams of making millions in the NFL one day, and I believe he will. Nonetheless, he is already one of the richest people I know. Rocky is one of the finest football players to ever play at OU, but he is an even finer young man. I have been truly blessed by knowing Rocky and his family and by having the opportunity to coach him. To say the least, it has been very refreshing. I'd like to thank Rocky for all he's done for the coaching staff, the University of Oklahoma, and me personally. We've all been made better because of our association with him, and I look forward to a lasting friendship.

CHAPTER ONE

Grandma, Please Stay

On August 1, 1979 while enduring a very hot summer day in Oklahoma, Linda Calmus began to have abdominal twinges and low back pain. She was very pregnant and felt as though she had feet like an elephant's. She was busy preparing a sit-down luncheon for her Kansas kinfolks when she felt the first twinge.

Matriarch Grandma Ayres said, "Oh, honey, you're just busy; when you slow down the pain will go away." Linda was feeling very emotional at the time since she was large, tired, and overdue. She really wanted her grandma to stay.

Great Grandma Ayres and Lance Calmus

Between frying the chicken and mashing the potatoes, the pain increased in intensity and duration. At one point she said, "Grandma, please stay. I'm going to have this baby." Linda would know since this was her fourth child. But no; her stubborn, German grandmother, Laura

Wilamina Langhofer-Ayres, had a frequent saying that she repeated: "Fish and company both begin to smell after three days." So Grandma and the other relatives packed their car and headed back to the little town of Herington, Kansas.

Myrle and nieces Dawn-Maire, and Kim finished the dishes as Linda's pains and groans increased. Six hours after some difficult labor in the hospital, Linda told her husband, "I don't know if I can do this Lamaze bite-the-bullet stuff; this really, really hurts."

Myrle patted Linda on the hand and said soothingly, "Now honey, you are doing good. You can make it."

"Oh, yeah, Myrle?" Linda said through her pain. "That's easy for you to say. Get the heck out of here!" She thought to herself, *I thought this was supposed to get easier!*

Feeling like a cavewoman, Linda endured without benefit of medications or injections, showing where Rocky gets his toughness. Her physician, Dr. Mulholland joined Myrle in guessing the baby's weight just like judges at a state fair. "9 pounds!" one said. "No, 10!" Little Rocky Ayres Calmus weighed in at a *mere* 11 pounds, 11 ounces—yes that is *pounds*—and was 21¾ inches long.

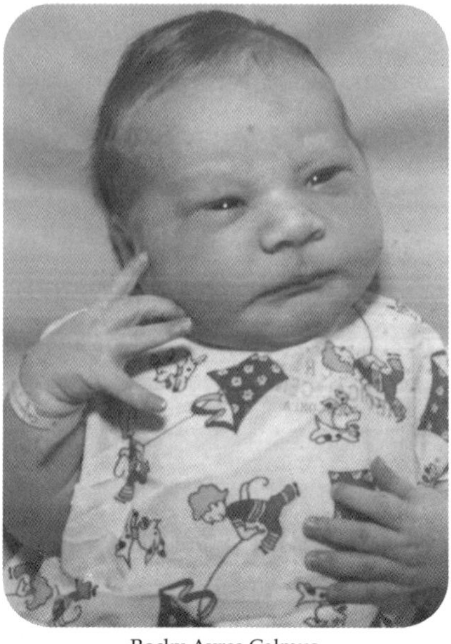

Rocky Ayres Calmus
11lb. 11oz -21¾ " long

Myrle described Rocky's arrival by saying, "He squirted out like a big pimple." What a lovely description.

Dr. Mulholland said, "I felt like I was catching a football." Could that have been an omen?

Rocky set a record for the largest Lamaze baby born in the Tulsa area at that time. With a head of blond hair, really big hands, and dark eyes, he looked like his big brother Lance. It's hard to tell their baby pictures apart.

All the Calmus kids were big babies. Lance, the oldest, weighed 9 pounds, 9 ounces; Richie was 10 pounds, and Mandy was 11 pounds, 5 ounces. But 11-11 topped them all!

Yes, his real name is Rocky. His dad named him that because he really did look like a prizefighter. No sissy names for this kid!

CHAPTER TWO

Tough Toddler

The first time the family realized Rocky had a high-pain tolerance was when he fell from a two-story home to the cement below. Family friends had a small balcony with wooden slats around their home. Rocky squeezed between the slats and fell about ten to twelve feet to the ground. Angels must have been protecting him, and the fall could have been fatal if he had gotten a head injury or a fractured skull. Instead, he had all the skin scraped off the side of his face, neck, and shoulder. Thank God it wasn't worse! Linda and Myrle got a lot of stares from people no doubt wondering, "Did you abuse this poor child?" As it healed, it did look pretty pathetic.

Rocky 2½ years old

Rocky always had a scrape when he was little, whether it was on his face, chin, arms, or legs. Now they are just bigger!

CHAPTER THREE

First Speeding Ticket

The Calmus clan spent many summer hours at various Oklahoma lakes. Myrle was a schoolteacher, and Linda was a school nurse—so June, July, and August were pretty free for the family to travel. The Calmus siblings all learned to water ski by age five, could swim like fish, and loved to make S'mores and foil dinners. From a tent to a Ford van to a 24-foot trailer, the camping got bigger and better. They were all avid skiers and boaters but poor fishermen, though Rocky seemed to always catch one or two. He loves to fish today but rarely has time.

Rocky driving the boat, Grandpa Ayres(standing), Lance (life jacket), Myrle

They never made lake trips on Sunday, but it always seemed that they were on a lake for August 1, Rock's birthday. The Calmus family celebrated Rocky's first four years with birthday cake at a lake. It was hard to keep ice cream frozen, but they made up for that with sparklers, presents, and festive party hats.

Rocky 3 years old. Annual birthday party at the lake.

On one of those trips, Rocky, then four, was speeding through the park on his mean green Hot Wheels machine when a park ranger pulled him over. Hiding a smile, he said, "Young man, you are exceeding the 5 mph posted speed limit." Busted!

CHAPTER FOUR

Cover Up Your Head

Linda and Richie, the second oldest, enjoyed trekking across Oklahoma on bicycles by the time he was seven years old. They made long trips that were endurance challenges, riding sixty to one hundred miles a day and camping out each night in a small Oklahoma town. The event, called Freewheel, made for a long, grueling week in June.

Rocky in kindergarten, biggest one in the group

As a school nurse at Glenpool, Linda rode fourteen miles from her home to work, going uphill but coasting on the way home. She was not ready to leave baby Rocky just yet, and since

Rocky had an early birthday, August 1, he was a young five for kindergarten. Linda arranged for a transfer and took baby Rock to his first class, right across from her nursing office.

Linda attached a two-wheel buggy to her bike and took the two of them to school every day. Rocky weighed less than fifty pounds at the time, but he was so embarrassed that he covered his head up with a blanket because he thought the kids would make fun of him.

Actually, most of the students thought it was neat that Nurse Calmus rode to school each day, setting a good example for health and exercise.

His music teacher, Bobbie Martin, one of the family's longtime friends, remembered those days. Bobbie says, "Rocky has been all boy, very normal—a very good young man." She admired that he always showed respect to his parents. Bobbie and her husband enjoyed being part of Rocky's high school graduation and his OU signing party. "His readiness to profess his faith in the Lord is just wonderful," she went on. Bobbie has always been proud of the way Rocky handled TV interviews with his realistic and direct comments.

Rocky with his music teacher, Bobbie Martin

She still laughs when she thinks of Rocky's chunky little body hiding under the blanket when his mom took him to school. She recalls asking him, "What are you doing, Rocky?"

Under his cover, he replied, "I'm covering up my head so no one will see me!"

CHAPTER FIVE

Sibling Rivalry at Its Best

Rocky, the youngest of four children, was given a lot of things—mostly hand-me-downs. He loved wearing his brothers' shirts, mostly the ones with a sports emblem or a number emblazed on the front. He didn't talk for the first three years of his life—didn't have to. His brothers and sister did everything for him. Sister Mandy treated him as her real live baby, but that didn't last too long. Soon he was the annoying little brother!

The following are some memories from his siblings' perspectives, beginning with Mandy Mae Calmus, his one and only sister:

Sister, Mandy Mae Calmus— The Good, the Bad, and the Ugly

I have a lot of fond memories of looking for bugs and snakes and stuff with Rock. Rocky was always the typical little brother—tag-along. At the time this was not cool, but it seemed like everywhere I went Rock went too, and I hated it!

He had a box he named Rocky's Bug Box, and we often went looking for snakes, tadpoles, and crawdads. We would lift the stock tank up, which was our pool at the time, and would catch grass snakes. Then we would go to the creek down by our house and turn over rocks to catch whatever was available. We would add all these critters to Rocky's Bug Box.

We used to love to tear up the house by making huge blanket tents together, and we shared a room. I had to cheer for him at ball games when I was a cheerleader, and this meant that he also went to our pizza parties! We played T-ball together, and I always had to go to the Jenks pool with him. We of course caught bugs together, and he even went to Camp Fire camp with me! Looking back now, these all ended up being good memories of my little bro.

When we were kids, we spent nearly every summer at the lake. We would always celebrate Rock's birthday there, and every birthday he would get a new Big Wheel—once he even got picked up by the park ranger for going too fast on it in the park! Every year, Richie and Rock would build me a new Big Wheel out of Rocky's salvaged ones. It was definitely the most colorful one because of all the mixed in parts (yellow handle bars, blue wheel up front, black wheels in back).

Mandy and Rocky

Like I said, Rocky and I even played T-Ball together. I was the only girl on the team, but you couldn't really tell because I had short hair. I was bigger than most of the boys, and I was better at it than Rock, too. I got to play first base because I was the only one who could catch the ball, and Rocky had to play outfield.

Every Christmas, especially since we shared a room and because the older boys wouldn't get up with him, Rock would wake me up at 4:00 or 5:00 in the morning to go down and see what Santa had brought for us. He was always the first up for Christmas morning, and we all really hated it that he got up so early. At least I never had to worry about over-sleeping, because Rock was up way before the sun was!

The Calmus family
Christmas Day

Rock and I loved to fish, so Mom would always take us fishing on Saturdays. If we were not able to drive a long distance, she would take us down to the Arkansas River. I remember she used to tell us we were just feeding the fish!

After I moved away from home and purchased my own house, everyone pitched in to paint and clean. Rock was extremely busy with football and college courses at OU, and I was surprised that he took the time to help. I was more shocked when Rocky ended up being one of the hardest workers. Of course, one of his jobs was knocking out the tile in my shower, which meant he could throw the sledgehammer around. He worked pretty hard that day and stayed for a long time. Thanks, Rock.

When I was young, Rocky saved my life. I'm sure it was a difficult thing for him to see and deal with, as it was for my entire family, but Rocky is the one who saved me, and I'm eternally thankful for that!

Looking back, I suppose there were some bad times, too. There were a lot of times when I would do something, such as break a window, and I'd blame it on Rocky. I remember that Richie also passed blame on to Rock. The crazy thing is, a lot of times Rocky just took the blame and went on. Poor Rocky got blamed for *many* things he didn't do!

There were times, due to the competitive nature of our family, that Richie and Rocky got into some nasty, knockdown, drag-out fights. It was scary to see this because it was like no one could really stop them from fighting. I remember one morning when I had stayed home from school that I heard a lot of yelling outside. I looked out my window and saw Richie, Rocky, Mom, and the neighbors, Tina and Vicki. My dad had already left for work, and they were all yelling and trying to break up Rich and Rock. They knocked down the chain link fence. Rocky, barefoot, kicked a big dent in Richie's Iroc. I recall Richie being sick at school later that day because Rocky had hit him on the head. I always hated to see them fight because that usually meant I had to kick some butt, too!

Rocky, 10 years old

Rock and I had some ugly times, too. My dad always disliked it when Rocky and I played basketball together out in the front driveway because he would have to break us up when we got into fistfights. We always felt that the other one was cheating. The competition was pretty fierce.

As I said earlier, Rocky and I had to share a room. He had the top bunk, and I had the bottom. It was terrible to have to share a room with my little brother. He always snored, and I would kick his bunk from below so he would roll over and quit snoring.

I remember that when Rocky was younger, he hated taking showers and we made fun of him for it. It seemed like every time you saw Rocky he was just a big, stinky, dirt ball. One summer he broke his foot and he had a cast on it, and man that thing was stinky! He would just go swimming in it and everything—he didn't care.

Rocky wanted to be like his older brothers in every way, and this meant he would pretty much copy anything they said, especially when it came to calling people bad names. Rocky was the worst at name-calling! He would always say that my lifelong friend Michelle and I had "big ole' butts." This hurt my feelings and made me so mad; we would usually end up fighting over this. Funny thing is, Rock now has something following him around as well.

One summer, Mom took Richie, Rock, and me to Disney World in Orlando, Florida. At one point, while we were at the Magic Kingdom, Rocky got mad at Mom and just took off. Somehow, we ended up passing him later on. He was lucky! With six thousand people in attendance and hundreds of acres of ground to cover, it was very scary because he was just ten years old. After finding him, Mom didn't know whether to hug or whip him.

It has been exciting to watch everything come together for Rocky. Even though Rock and I spent a lot of time together when we were younger, as we grew older, we also grew apart. Everything that has happened with him in football has helped bring our family closer. It has also given us a lot of opportunities to do fun, exciting things and to meet new people. A great example was when we all went to the Butkus Awards together. We had such an awesome time! Lance, Rich, Teri, and I all had a blast at Universal Studios. The awards ceremonies for ESPN, the Butkus Awards, and the Orange Bowl are events that few people get to experience firsthand. Rocky's success has allowed us to do things many people only imagine. What a trip it has been! I feel extremely lucky and am proud of Rock and my family.

The Calmus name brings wide eyes, stares, and always a question or two. I'm proud to answer, "Yes, Rocky's my little brother," and "Really! I'm not kidding!"

Brother, Richie Calmus

What can I say about my baby brother Rocky? I don't know where to start; there are so many things about Rocky I could say. I've gotten to watch him grow up from a dirty little boy that hated to take a bath to a strong young man.

Rocky was the youngest of us four kids and was the toughest little brother I knew. I remember one time that we took apart a dryer, and on the inside there was a big round steel barrel that held the clothes. We put pillows and blankets in it, and then we put little Rocky in, too. We rolled Rocky all around the neighborhood, slamming him into everything except moving cars. He loved it, and we laughed our heads off. He was the only one brave enough to do it.

I can remember playing flag football. Rocky wanted to play so badly, that my coach actually let him play with us.

Rocky's first year of tackle football, he showed up to practice with plastic shoulder pads and plastic Dallas Cowboys football helmet—the kind you buy at Wal-Mart. And I'll never forget the brown jeans he wore without pads. The coach told him that he needed *real* football equipment to play.

Rocky also loved bugs, snakes, frogs, and whatever he could find down at the creek. He used to carry a little box around that said "Rocky's Bug Box" on it. He filled it up with whatever moved. There are so many funny stories about Rocky when he was younger, but that would be another book.

Watching Rocky play sports in grade school, I knew he was going to be good. He was just so dominant on the field, court, or diamond.

Our family has been really blessed athletically. My uncle and father both signed with the Dodgers in 1963. Lance signed with the Cleveland Indians, and I signed up to play college football with a small school in Oklahoma. We all were All-Staters and Rock, Dad, and Uncle Richard were All-Americans. And you can't forget about Mandy, a cheerleader and great basketball player—and probably the toughest out of all of us. And of course there's Mom, who gave birth to four wonderful (and large) children.

Rocky, 6th grade Quaterback Club

Where did Rock get number twenty? He got it

from me. I was always number twenty growing up, and he wanted to be just like me. I recently read in a college magazine where a reporter asked Rock who he looked up to, and he said his older brothers and his father. That made me feel special!

In high school, Rock was the best player and number one pick in Oklahoma. I loved to watch him play, but I didn't get to very often because I was in college football myself. I remember that his senior year in high school I was in Durant, Oklahoma, at Southeastern State, which is two and a half hours away. I skipped curfew and drove to watch Rock play Union and then drove right back.

Lance, Richie, Mandy, and Rocky

The last couple of years have been so much fun for our family and Rock. Now that I've graduated from college, I've gotten to watch him a lot, and it's been awesome watching him dominate the line of scrimmage. There are two plays that I remember most clearly. The first was an interception from Chris Simms where he returned it for a touchdown in the OU/Texas game. The second was the hit on Heismen Trophy winner Chris

Weinke that caused a fumble that OU recovered, enabling them to win the National Championship.

After winning the Big XII Championship game, Rocky came to the stands and gave me a hug. A photographer captured the moment, and I have that picture hanging on my wall.

Over the last couple of years, we have gotten a lot closer. Our family is a loving, close, Christian family, and Rock and I have been able to spend a lot more time together. We have taken road trips, and we didn't even get into a single fight! We spent a lot of time at the lake learning to wakeboard.

The summer of 2001 was the most fun. It was the funniest thing to watch Mandy and me trying to hit that little white golf ball. Rock, being the "professional" golfer, kept trying to show us, but we were helpless.

Rock has been so good to me. He gets my female friends tickets for the games. We all go out after the games and eat, watch movies, play golf, or just hang out. Rocky is a very giving person. Our family has gotten to experience so many great opportunities over the years, and it has been so much fun—the Independence Bowl, the Big XII Championship game, the Orange Bowl, the Butkus Awards in Florida where we met Dick Butkus, and simple things like tailgate parties with our family and friends.

I'm proud of Rocky because of what he stands for and his commitment to his beliefs. I think his success is a tribute to my parents and the way they have raised Rocky and all of us. They are great parents, and I think it reflects in the way we've turned out. I thank the Lord every day for our family and how much we've been blessed.

Brother, Lance Calmus

I'm of course the oldest, the best-looking, the smartest, and the best athlete of the Calmus family. Now we know that's not true, or I would have a book about me, and I would have money and fame!

Well, I *am* the oldest. I'm six years older than Rock, so much of the time I was off doing my thing and Rock was doing his thing—which was, for years, eating dirt. That's one thing I—and all of my buddies—remember about Rock.

When I played sports, he would be over in the corner playing cup ball, football, or whatever game he could come up with. When he was not playing games, he was playing in the dirt—throwing it in the air, in his mouth, or at other kids. And usually when he was done with the dirt, he would find a frog and chase girls.

I also remember that Mom got us passes to the local swimming pool, which was just a few blocks down the road, during the summer. We often spent every day, all day long, there. Anyway, Rock wanted to jump off the high dive, which was ten feet high or higher. He was a little scared, so I told him I would be right below him on the side of the pool and that I would help him if he needed me. So he tiptoed out to the edge, looked down, and started back to the ladder.

You have to jump, Rocky!

I yelled at him, "You have to jump! Once you're up there you are not allowed to climb back down!" So he made his way back to the edge, got up the nerve, and jumped. But instead of jumping straight, he jumped to the side—right at me and the side of the pool, barely missing both by inches! It scared me more than it scared him. But from that jump on, it was nothing but the high dive for him, and he didn't even want my help anymore.

Being the youngest, Rock got picked on and teased a lot (something I would not advise doing now). We often picked on him about how bad his feet and shoes smelled. It was so bad, we would make him put his shoes outside so we wouldn't get sick! He just kind of shrugged it off, like it was no big deal. But one thing that was a big deal to him and would hurt his feelings was when we teased him about his lisp. He had trouble pronouncing some words, so we would tease him, and he would get so mad that there were some pretty good fights. I know it was a mean thing to do, but we were young kids.

Another thing Rock got for being the youngest was our hand-me-downs—old pants, shirts, shoes, etc.—so he always looked a little ragged. But there were a few advantages to being the youngest, one of which was that Richie, Mandy, and myself already had Mom and Dad broken in, so Rock got away with everything! Also, as the baby of the family, he would do the same thing one of us had done previously, but our parents' response would be, "He's only five," or, "He's only eight," all the way up until, "Don't worry about it, Lance, he's only fourteen."

I think one reason Rock is so tough is all the roughhousing that went on when we were younger. I remember we used to go down the road to a friend's house to jump on his trampoline. We played this game called Crack the Egg. We had one kid that would pull his knees to his chest and wrap his arms around himself. Then the rest of us jumped up and down really close to him and tried to pop him up high into the air—to crack the egg. As one might guess, Rock was always the egg. One time we really cracked him good, and I thought we had really hurt him badly. We popped him so high that Rock was at eye level with us while we were in the air. When he came down, he landed right on his head! I thought he'd broken his neck. He cried for about five minutes, but then he wanted to do it again. That's when I knew how tough—or how crazy—he was!

Another thing I remember about Rock is that while we were growing up, he always wanted to tag along. He always wanted to go everywhere with me. We did a lot of things together, but every once in a while it would annoy me that my little brother had to go with me. Then other times he could not go, and it would make me feel bad that he wanted to go so badly; he'd stand in the yard, reaching out his arms and crying out, "I want to go," as we drove off. It would often put me in a sad mood for half the time I was gone.

It's kind of funny—I'm the one tagging along with him now! But I wouldn't change a thing, though I would have liked to have been at more of his games. I couldn't be any more proud of him! I'm not only proud of him for all of his on-field accomplishments but also for all the things he does off the field and for his commitment and values.

He's a good Christian, a great person, a wonderful brother, and a terrific uncle to my son Tucker.

I love him very much and I am very proud to be his big brother!

CHAPTER SIX

Tough Teenager, Tough Knocker

Rocky's sister, Mandy, tells a story about she and Rocky riding the old green moped together. Myrle had told them, "I don't want you two to ride together. You'll get hurt." But of course they did, and of course they had a crash. Rocky hurt his shoulder but was afraid to say anything. About two hours after he went to bed, he finally came in and woke his parents—trip to the emergency room number ninety-nine (not really) where an x-ray revealed Rock's shoulder blade was fractured.

Rocky and namesake, Grandpa Ayres
Lance, Richie (front)

The next big injury (there were a lot of little ones) was when Rocky was about twelve. While playing baseball, Rocky was rounding third and ran into home base, twisting his ankle. He limped around for three days while his mother was out of town. When Linda called home and heard that his ankle was still very swollen—despite the fact that Rocky wasn't complaining much—she said, "Get that kid to the ER now!" It wasn't serious—he'd only fractured his ankle in *three* separate places.

Back: Richie, Lance
Front: Mandy, Rocky

As most of his OU fans know, Rocky has had a separated shoulder, deep thigh bruise, his rib cage cartilage torn, multiple groin pulls, hamstrings, sprains, strains, hip pointers, and various other little injuries, but he plays through them all.

In 1999, he fractured his right thumb, continued to play in a soft cast, and was treated with a bone stimulator (to promote healing) for three months. In 2000, he fractured his left thumb and wore a long arm cast for the entire year.

Perhaps the most publicized story was his fractured tibia during the Texas Tech game in 1999. The airplane had mechanical trouble, so the team rode in a cramped bus with Rocky's leg hanging down. After eight hours in that position, his leg looked *terrible* from the swelling, discoloration, and poor circulation.

The big in-state rival game with OSU was the following week, and was OU's last game of the season. Rocky said he might play. Linda could not believe her ears! She pleaded, "Please, Rocky, don't risk a greater injury!"

Rocky responded by saying that if he gave the thumbs up sign, he would play. He said, "If I'm walking, I'm playing. I can't ride the sideline."

Linda's mouth fell open when she saw Rocky's thumb pointing up during warm ups. Her eyes watered, and she wanted to scream at the coach and doctor. In their defense, Rocky was a big part of the scenario. College games are different, and they do require, if it's at all possible, for the kids to suck it up and play. So after no practice for a week, Rocky played against OSU like a madman for three quarters.

Three days after OU's National Championship, Rocky had his right wrist fused with a bone graft taken from his hip. No one knew that he had pulled the ligaments away from his right thumb during the Texas game, either—he had a cast with the thumb extended for four weeks. Coach Stoops did not publicize all of the team's injuries, and that was for the players' protection.

Left to right, Richie,Lance, Mandy, and Rocky

Coach Venables called Rocky "a tough knocker" who has his respect. "I haven't been around someone [before] who can fight through that much pain."

Teammate Roy Williams said, "You'd have to tie Rocky up and lock him in somewhere to keep him from playing—and then he'd break free. His desire on the field is unbelievable, and I respect him as a player for that."

Mike Stoops once said, "Rocky is our leader by example in his toughness and his competitiveness, and that has rubbed off. Rocky's toughness is a lot like Josh Heupel's leadership on offense."

The Calmus brothers Richie, Rocky, and Lance

I guess it is a good thing Rocky is tough because a former pro-football player told his family, "Rocky's hardest hit…in the toughest college game will be routine in daily practice at the NFL."

Rocky actually seemed to get hurt more during the time he played baseball and basketball in junior high and high school than he did while playing football. It might have had something to do with the fact that in basketball he was all over the floor, diving for loose balls, driving for the hoop at full speed, and going for rebounds with two or three guys pounding on him. Considering all the contact in football, the protective gear must help out a lot.

Rocky gives his mom the credit for his endurance: "I get my toughness from mom. She had me without any medicine, and I weighed eleven pounds, eleven ounces. I guess that's pretty big."

CHAPTER SEVEN

Tales and Tidbits from Family and Friends

When Linda Calmus and family friend Mary Engles decided to put together a book about Rocky, they sat down and wrote a letter to friends and family members, asking them to share their memories of Rocky. They asked for the good, the bad, the ugly, as well as anything they thought was funny, unusual, or exciting. Though they received lots of responses, there were some entries that didn't make it before the deadline as the book went to print. Those included below, however, include some fun stories from family members, friends, neighbors, and coaches, beginning with Rocky's girlfriend and high school sweetheart, Teri Marcum.

High school sweetheart, Teri Marcum

Rocky was on a Young Life retreat in North Carolina—a neat place called Windy Gap. He had come home after meeting some new friends there, and those friends happened to be my friends—some really good friends, and that's how we met.

This was in July of 1996, and we all hung out together the rest of the summer. At that time, we were just friends. Rocky was sweet but very shy, which is hard to imagine *now*, and he had very little confidence with girls.

High school sweetheart Teri Marcum

We were going to separate high schools—I went to Memorial and Rocky attended Jenks. But I saw something special in him; he was a great friend and a very caring person.

We stayed friends for about three months through phone conversations and by chatting after practice, etc. I slowly began to see a different side of Rock. He became more confident, his shyness subsided (some), and he became more outgoing. Somewhere in the middle of this change, I fell in love.

Our relationship officially began on November 3, 1996. Most people thought this was just a high school crush, but I knew differently. I knew Rocky was the One, and as I write this, we've just celebrated the fifth anniversary of our relationship. I am surer of our love every day.

Our junior and senior years of high school mainly consisted of sports, sports, and more sports. He played football, basketball, and baseball. I played soccer, basketball, and club soccer year round. We only had time together between games and practices.

We were both captains of our high school teams, and we each received All-State Awards; we both won a State

Championship our senior years. We both signed with Big XII schools on the same day—me to OSU, Rock to OU.

I gave Rocky a darling, big brown-eyed Boxer puppy for our third anniversary. He is a big responsibility when we both have to go in different directions for the weekend, but he is our baby. We named the dog Owen Butkus because Rocky didn't want to call the dog by saying, "Here Butkus!" His first name, Owen, comes from Owen Field, of course, and Butkus from the Butkus Award, which has always been one of Rocky's goals. Owen Butkus Calmus is a very special dog, and he is quite spoiled.

Teri and Rocky with puppy "Owen Butkus"

Rocky and I are both very strong Christians. We love the Lord very much and are thankful for each day He gives us and every blessing He puts in our lives. We both hold each other accountable, and we have given each other a lot of stability and consistency in our daily walk of faith. Rocky and I once even had the opportunity to share our faith at a youth rally called True Love Waits.

Our faith has matured in college as we have grown up together. We found a church we love, Emmaus Baptist, which has become a big part of our life. The preacher, Mike Booth, and his wife Freddy have been friends and mentors to us. We have

Teri Marcum and Rocky

dinner together frequently, and Rocky and Pastor Booth play golf every chance they get.

I have seen Rocky grow and change a lot in the past couple of years. Although he may not be the most vocally outspoken person when it comes to his faith, it's not difficult to see his values by how he lives. I truly believe his values are a big part of why he has been so blessed.

Family friend, Beverly Henderson

I remember Rocky as a little boy with very blond hair and an ability to avoid anything undesirable by disappearing before detection. He was quiet, but he seemed to have trouble staying still. Rocky never seemed to be a demanding child, wanting to play in an imaginary world of sports heroes. Little did we know that he would one day become the great player he imagined himself to be.

Aunt and Uncle, Cindy and John Musgrove

We have made so many fond memories of all the Calmus kids over the years. We had many good times camping in our tent at the lake. Rocky was always a tormentor, and his passion was getting my hair wet while we were swimming. Of course, I especially told him not to, but that was Rocky—pester, pester.

Our Christmases were always special. We had a great Santa that came every year—tall kids sitting on Santa's lap made for some cute pictures—and I especially remember the year the boys got their lettermen jackets.

At Easter, I always made very large cookies with lots of icing, and everyone got one with his name on it. Rocky always wanted more than one and tried to get anyone to give him another!

My family and I have followed the Calmus kids through all their sports, starting with Lance, the oldest Calmus brother, as he played baseball and football at Jenks. Then there were Richie's great football years at Jenks and his college games and Mandy's basketball at Jenks. Finally, there's Rock—he's been instrumental in so many games. We thought the two Jenks championship games were about the best there could be. None of that, though, compares to the National Championship Orange Bowl he played in Florida.

We've had so much fun watching the college games, going to the tailgate parties, and traveling to the away games as a family. We've even rented a large van a couple of times so that ten of us could laugh and talk and replay the games together.

I think it's neat that the players go around the stadiums thanking their fans. At the big win over Texas in 2000, we were lucky enough to draw first row seats in the end zone. After the game, Rocky saw us and came over. We got hugs, and ESPN captured the moment—an experience I'll never forget. After that, I was known as Rocky's "TV Mom," since Linda and I look somewhat alike.

Season ticket holders Uncle John, Aunt Cindy, Cousin Dawn

It's hard to believe our little Tormentor has turned into such a great talent on the football field. But above all that, his lifestyle off the field is more memorable. His high morals, the kindness he especially shows to kids wanting autographs, and the spiritual leadership he demonstrates to all the players makes us even more proud of him.

He owes a lot to his parents for the values they instilled in him. I know he'll take all this to the next level, and as a family, we'll be there.

Cousin, Dawn Musgrove

My fiancé, Richard Fain, has two boys, and everyone has accepted them with open arms—especially Rocky.

The first time Brandon and Dylan Fain met Rocky was at his parent's house. I was so impressed with the way Rocky warmed up to the boys. Before the day was over, Rocky was outside playing football with both of them. Brandon actually intercepted the ball when Rocky was the one who was supposed to catch it! Rocky has always been good with kids. I think that is what I respect most about him. There are many children who look up to him, and he has always made time for all of them. Meeting Rocky has made a huge impact on Brandon and Dylan. I wish that I could have met someone when I was their age that I could have idolized as much as they do Rocky.

However, I will always remember Rocky as being a pest and always picking on everyone. A great example is Thanksgiving Day 2001, when Rocky was running through the house with a wet terry towel and popping people on the butt. Will he ever change?

I had season tickets to OU, and the four years have passed so quickly. It has been a whirlwind of fun, and Rocky has made it all possible. I am in special education, and Rocky has signed several items for my Special Kids Too program. Rocky is always ready, willing, and able to be there for the less fortunate.

Thanks, Cuz!

Cousins, John and Radonn Musgrove

When reflecting on my memories and thoughts about Rocky, I can recall feeling that Rocky had that extra-special ability and talent. I remember going to see him play football when he was in the fourth or fifth grade; he was a team leader then, also. He'd jump right up from a tackle and pat somebody on the back for doing a good job.

Being a graduate of OU and a big OU football fan, I was happy that John and I got to take Richie and Rocky to their first OU game. However, OU lost and performed terribly, and I didn't think Rocky would come back to play ball there.

I know Rocky was under extreme pressure from lots of people regarding his choice of colleges. I really prayed that he'd attend OU because of a feeling in my heart that he was an exceptional person and a ball player destined for greatness. I truly believe that he is one of the reasons that OU's football program has returned to greatness. I had a dream that my father told me I shouldn't worry, that Rocky would go to OU. My dad's name was Ron (Coach Gibbs' father is also named Ron), and I have heard Coach Gibbs talk about feeling the presence of his father during the rebirth of OU football. I truly believe these two Rons whispered in God's ear to get Rocky to OU!

I cannot say enough about how much I admire Linda and Myrle because of the way they shaped the behavior and personalities of their children. All of them are very kind to my children, all four possess wonderful athletic gifts, and above all, they are wonderful people.

I can think of many kind deeds Rocky has done for others, but a couple really stand out in my mind. The first one was when I was very ill during my pregnancy with my daughter, Sloane. Rocky had just told his parents where he had decided to attend college, and knowing his decision would lift my spirits, he called and told me he had decided on OU. This really touched my heart and made me feel so much better.

Rocky also took the time one day to come spend the afternoon with my kindergarten class. I had a student that really needed some encouragement, and Rocky made him his special helper. Needless to say, unselfish, kind acts like these produced far-reaching effects that can never be measured.

I can say that I have never once seen Rocky scoff at giving an autograph or a kind word to an adoring fan. Through all this excitement, he has stayed the same person we know and love.

Uncle and Aunt, Mike and Althea Adams

At about age six, Rocky was visiting our farm in Okmulgee. His Grandpa Oscar, Uncle Mike, and Aunt Althea were building a playhouse for the kids. Rocky asked if he could let the chickens out of their pen, and Mike said sure. We sat back to watch the excitement. It wasn't long after that we saw a streak running across the yard and a shrill voice saying, "Grannnnndpaaaaaa, he's after me!" The rooster was on Rocky's heels, and he was running for all he was worth. After all the laughter was over, we knew we had a star in the family—the rooster didn't catch Rock.

On another occasion down on the farm, Rocky was riding horses with his cousin Jared. The two had been riding for a while when a rabbit jumped out from under the bushes. The next thing Jared heard was Rocky trying to calm his horse. He looked back to see Rocky emerge from under the cloud of dirt, running after his horse. The two of them finally caught up with the horse and decided Rocky wasn't quite ready for a John Wayne movie yet.

Rocky is a very family-oriented person. One of Rock's favorite pastimes is pestering, but that's just Rocky.

We've all watched with pride, excitement, and joy at Rock's talent and accomplishments over the years. A lot has already been written about those achievements. Rocky always gives credit to his teammates, his coaches, and most of all, his God. Linda and Myrle instilled high values in him early on. Proverbs 22:6 says, "Train up a child in the way he should go, and when he is old, he will not turn from it."

The kind of person we decide to be will affect every area of our lives. Rocky chose to continue the path his parents set forth, and his humbleness and love for the Lord is a true testament to his character. His moral standards on and off the field are exemplary.

As I sit here recalling the memories with smiles and tears, please know, Rocky, you have enriched all our lives as well as many others. Thanks for being such a fine young man. You are a winner in every aspect! Whatever path you choose, we are here to support, love, and share in the memories yet to come.

Kansas Relatives (and big K-State Fans), Muriel and Wilbur Ihde

We, "the Kansans," often think what a team member K-State would have had with a *Rocky Calmus*! We also wish him well in the future, and we are proud of his accomplishments and the Christian attitude he has shown by his decisions. We know he has enjoyed his association with the Sooners.

Neighbor, Doris Vivian

Linda and Myrle Calmus moved to a home across the street from me about twenty-nine years ago. I saw every little Calmus soon after he or she arrived into this world. It was the same when Rocky made his appearance—another little neighbor that I went to see—the new *big* bundle of joy at the hospital. He was surrounded by loving family and friends, as is still the case. Everyone that was gathered had to agree that the name Myrle picked for his new baby boy was very fitting. As he grew to a rough and tumble boy, his name matched perfectly.

There were seventeen boys of various ages living on our little street. Rocky's older brothers, Lance and Richie, were the same age as my son. As a whole, all of these boys played together very well. Occasionally, his big brothers would permit Rocky to tag along for the day's play. It seems I was usually cooking when all of these boys visited my house. Lance and Rocky would come into the kitchen to check on my efforts and to ask, "What are you cooking?"

I always felt appreciated. I would lift a lid from a pan of food and hear a big "Uummmm" from Rocky.

It has been a pleasure to watch Rocky grow from a little boy to a young man. I've spent many hours watching him play high school football for Jenks, then many additional hours for Oklahoma University.

People often ask me about Rocky Calmus. I'm always pleased to reply, "He's my neighbor." I'm most proud of the qualities he carries in his heart off the football field.

Neighbors, Vicki and Tina Rowland

We have known the Calmus family since Rocky was about nine months old. When we moved next door to them, Tina, our daughter, was twelve years old. Her first thought when she saw baby Rocky was *babysitting,* which she got to do!

The Calmus boys and girl were always good kids. You didn't see as much fighting as you would with most brothers. They were always courteous and sweet—except for one morning when Tina and I were in our car heading to work, and I saw Linda Calmus outside trying to stop Rocky and Richie from fighting it out! I stopped the car in the middle of the street and got out to help her. Here Tina and I were, between two very big boys, trying to dodge the punches. We finally separated them and they each went on their way. That evening they were home and back to the loving and caring brothers I know. It seems that no matter what happens between them, they are always there for each other—no matter what.

We followed Rocky through Jenks football and watched him sign autographs and talk with the younger children. Even then, Rocky was an idol to them. We have had the privilege of following him through his college years at Oklahoma University, and still he signs autographs and is a roll model to children and adults alike. He always has the time after a game to give us a big hug and thank us for coming to watch him play.

Rocky, when you chose OU, I know Ray (my late husband) was shouting "Amen!" in heaven, since that was always his team. I know he is as proud of you today as we are. You have given us the most memorable years of our lives. The times we shared with your family on road trips to the away OU football games have meant so much. It has been such fun and a pure pleasure. We love you!

Friend, Mary Engles

My favorite Rocky memory brings to mind a cool spring afternoon with the sun shining brightly. My three elementary-age children were resting after lunch, watching cartoons, when I heard shouting and a loud commotion coming from outside. Skinny, lanky, Rocky came running across my front yard and headed for my front porch, his two older brothers not far behind. Rock was shouting, "Help me, help me! They're gonna get me!"

Once Rocky reached the protection of my front porch, he pleaded, "Mrs. Engles, don't let them get me!" His brothers stopped by my fence when they saw Rocky hide behind my back in the safety of the front porch. Rich and Lance wouldn't come any closer, but taunted Rock by saying, "You can't stay on that porch forever. We're gonna get you for what you've done." Rock poked his head out from behind my back and stuck out his tongue at his big brothers and laughed. He was safe now and back to old cocky Rocky. Richie and Lance headed home, and Rock stayed and played. I never found out what "sweet" Rocky did to cause such a ruckus!

Mary Engles, Rocky, and Rob Engles

My son, Dillon Engles, played football with Rocky since they were in fifth grade. Some of my fondest memories of Rocky were actually through my son. Rocky was always the star in football, the one who carried the ball and ran over and around everyone for touchdowns. My son was an offensive lineman. After a big win, Rocky was the one interviewed by the news media, but he would not take all the glory. He gave praise to the linemen who opened the holes for him to dart through. He always recognized that it took *teamwork* and not just one player to win the games. Even though he was a head taller than most players, much faster, and more talented, he still acknowledged the good plays of the offensive linemen. This left a strong positive image on Dillon and encouraged him to work even harder at making those blocks for Rock.

My photography brings us to OU football and Rocky Calmus. I have taken pictures of Richie, Rocky, and my sons Dillon and Nathan playing sports together since elementary school. When Rocky went to OU, I photographed my son Dillon's college football career for two years until injury kept him from playing. Then I transferred to taking pictures of OU football. The Jenks Journal requested my OU sideline photography pass from OU.

During Rocky's senior year at OU, I was able to follow his career through the eye of my camera. It was a memorable year, catching all the action from the sidelines. Linda Calmus and her sister, Cindy, planned and provided tailgate parties for all the home games. After Rocky signed autographs, he enjoyed some good chow and relaxation time after a hard game.

Some of my best memories of Rocky and OU football are the thrill I experienced walking through the tunnel and out into the open field at the Cotton Bowl, the excitement I felt on entering the media tent along with numerous TV cameras and sports reporters after the big win over Texas, and the scare watching a rocket football land and bounce right next to my foot. On another occasion, I was watching a play through the camera lens and didn't see these huge linemen coming from the side—the play crashed in front of me, and I rolled over backwards, trying to protect my camera. I was on TV with my feet up in the air, rolling over backwards—a really respectable view! I enjoyed listening firsthand to Rock's interviews outside the locker rooms after each game. I will never forget the jubilation I felt when Rock motioned for me to run with him, with the team right behind, back out on the field for team pictures with the trophy after the Red River Shootout. I'll always recall the pleasure I felt when Rocky saw me after games, with camera in tow and looking for that great picture, and would oblige with a pause and a smile.

Mary Engles, Photographer

Linda and Myrle Calmus, Tina and Vicki Rowland, John and Cindy Musgrove, Doris Vivian and I were regulars at the away games, and we'd usually visit Rocky in his hotel room the night before a game. At the Red River Shootout game in Texas, we weren't sure where his hotel room was located. He told Linda that he was at the Marriott by the airport, but he wasn't sure where the hotel was. We drove to the airport, but none of us realized how large an area that is. We said a quick prayer for guidance, and guess what pulled up right in front of us—a Marriott transport bus! We followed close behind as the bus stopped at each station at the airport, letting passengers off and on. The bus led us through the traffic and around expressways right to the Marriott where Rocky was staying. We arrived as Rocky called again on Linda's cell phone, asking if we were going to make it.

On one such visit to Rocky's hotel rooms, a young boy was just outside Rocky's room looking for autographs from players. He didn't even know he was right by Rock's room! I told him I could get an autograph and took his ball into Rock's room. Instead of signing the ball and handing it back to me to return to the young man, Rock got up, went into the hallway, and knelt down by the boy. He asked his name and personalized the autograph. The jubilant boy ran down the hall to his dad and yelled, "I got a good one! I got *Rocky's* signature!"

I remember the warm feeling I got when Linda told me that he worried about me when I missed a game. I think his statement was, "Where's Mary? She's fired as my personal photographer!" Rocky, without you I wouldn't have been a sports photographer and could not have enjoyed the limelight of OU football from the sideline.

Thanks, Rock!

Family friends, Max and Sandra Ridgeway

Our fond memories of Rocky as a child begin with the toddler. We remember Rocky as a stout, vivacious, and tow-headed boy with a name that suited him well. Our son Brad and Rocky's brother Lance played lots of sports together and were good friends. After spending the night with Lance when they were around nine or ten, Brad came home describing his experience at the Calmus household by saying, "Mom, that place is something! Lance and I were asleep, and Rocky came in and jumped right on top of us! He is a strong little dude."

Our lives were intertwined with sports for several years as Lance and Brad played baseball and football together.

We moved to Houston in 1983, but then to our pleasant surprise, we were reintroduced to a grown-up Rocky at age eighteen. While visiting our family in Tulsa at Christmas, during Rocky's senior year of high school, our niece Teri brought Rocky for a family gathering.

Rocky and Teri started coming to Houston to visit us during spring break their freshman year of college. Like most college students, they had little money for vacations, so we had the pleasure of their company.

The spring of 2001, they came again to visit. We learned that Rocky was going to be participating in some benefit golf tournaments in Oklahoma, so we offered a golf lesson with the neighborhood golf pro, Mark Massengale. Since Rocky had just had surgery on his wrist after OU's wins at the Orange Bowl and the National Championship, we inquired about the effect swinging a golf club would have on his wrist. We didn't know that Rocky had been brought to his knees by a blow to his wrist in a playful encounter with one of Brad's children. Thankfully it was nothing serious, so a golf lesson was in order.

In the span of just a few days, Rocky took two golf lessons, hit numerous buckets of balls, and played a few holes on the course. We sent Rocky home with some old clubs. After a few weeks, we heard that a golf monster had been released in him. By the time we saw Rocky again Memorial Day weekend in Houston, he had a nice set of clubs and was playing golf at every opportunity. Now we knew what activities to line up for him during his visits. No more Astro World or fishing—just golf!

Rocky loves our home so much, he said he'd love to live in Brentwood, which might make the expansion team in Houston a good fit for him.

We believe that God brings people and circumstances into our lives for a *purpose*. We are thankful for the wonderful times that our relationship with Rocky has brought to our lives. He is a fine, upstanding Christian young man who is modest and genuine. What finer qualities could one desire?

Friends, Kathy, Jim, and Brett Butler

Our stories of Rocky dated back to the time that he and our son Brett were in the fourth grade. Rocky was a gangly little boy who was always busy, and Brett was his best buddy and sidekick. Brett looked to Rocky for athletic advice, while Rock looked to Brett for advice with the girls. Even as early as the fourth grade, Jim and I knew that Rocky would be where he is today. He was a natural.

Jim coached Rocky from the time he was in the fourth grade until he went into school ball in the eighth grade. Funny as it may seem now, we were really serious about football even then, and Rocky was our shining star. Jim puts it best when he says, "Rocky just has a nose for the ball; he is like a big old Lab going to a bone. He always knows where the ball is." A Labrador's personality is very similar to Rocky's; he was always frisky, friendly, and active.

When we were coaching the fifth grade, most boys were still learning to "take a knee," but we knew that we could just hand the ball off to Rock and he would drag tacklers at least five yards a carry. Jim would often say, "I'm just going to run Rocky right at them, and if they can stop him, I guess they're a better team." That really never happened, because we only lost one game from the fifth grade to the seventh grade.

At the end of Rocky's fifth grade year, we were undefeated and got a trophy about the size of the boys. Rocky still talks about that trophy every time he comes over; he is truly still a kid at heart.

Every year, our biggest rival was Short's team, and we always worried that they would ruin our undefeated season. One year, we almost got beaten because we tried something new. I'll never forget that game; we were sitting in the stands when all of a sudden Linda said to me, "You've got to come with me to the bathroom, I think I'm having a heart attack!" All of this for a seventh grade football game! As a postscript, Short's team never did beat us, and Linda did not have a heart attack.

Richie Calmus, Myrle Calmus, Rocky Calmus,
Head Coach Jim Butler, Ryan Butler, Brett Butler
Jenks Quarterback Club President, Rob Engles, Nate Engles, Dillon Engles

Every game from the time Rock was in the fourth grade until he went into school ball, he had to make weight in order to run with the ball. We would get him to our house, usually on Thursday, and he would stay with us until at least after the game on Saturday so that we could monitor his weight. I'll never forget his comment when we won our final game in the seventh grade, and he no longer had to weigh in. He said to me, "Kathy, just think; I can eat whatever I want now because I never have to weigh in again!"

Even at that age, Rocky truly took football seriously, and he took his responsibility and role in the team seriously. He was very committed and disciplined even then. Rocky never missed practice; it was truly a game to him, and he had fun. He always gave 110 percent, and even though he was truly the most gifted athlete on the field, he never slacked or expected any special treatment. He placed very high expectations on himself, and he always lived up to them. Rocky has always been happiest with the ball in his hand.

Little league was really fun, and it wasn't long ago that Rocky came over and he and Brett watched their little league highlight tapes all over again. He said to Brett, "You know, it's really a job now. We had so much fun then."

Once the boys went into school ball, they played for the Jenks Trojans, and it was such a source of pride for us. We had the "Legion of Doom," which has been dubbed by many people as the best defensive team that high school football in Oklahoma has ever seen.

Probably the biggest highlight I remember from their high school careers happened in the state semi-finals against Midwest City. Brett came home during the week and said, "You won't believe it, but we are putting in the Butler-Calmus connection." The Butler-Calmus connection was a halfback pass from Rocky to Brett that we had used and scored on since the fourth grade. Brett always said that Rocky could throw a mile, but you had to just watch where it was going because you were never sure; it would always go long, though.

I didn't pay much attention to Brett, because I knew that many times things that were practiced were never actually used in a game. But right before halftime, Jenks was behind. The boys were in a huddle and Rocky was warming his arm up. I looked to Jim and said, "They're getting ready to do that play!" I knew because every time we had ever run it, Rocky warmed his arm up in the huddle. Sure enough, they broke the huddle and Rocky launched a rocket to Brett—and he caught it for a touchdown! Rocky's dad *was* always convinced he should've been a quarterback. That one play totally changed the momentum of the game, and we went on to win that game and the State Championship that year.

Brett and Rocky completed high school with two state titles under their belt, and the team went down in history as the greatest high school football team in Oklahoma and ranked in the top ten nationally.

Oh, and did Rocky play hurt? I am amused when I hear people talk about how tough Rocky is and how he plays through injury, as if that is something new. Rocky has *always* played hurt. He was so active and so busy that something was always dinged up—so much so that many times, he didn't even know it. In the fourth grade, Rocky came home from football practice one day, and Linda noticed that he was sitting in front of the TV with a blanket over his shoulder. She found it a little odd, because one thing Rocky didn't do was sit. When he was still there a few hours later, she took the blanket off of his shoulder and found that he had broken his collarbone; this was after he had already been practicing that way for a few days!

Rocky is tough on the outside but he is truly soft on the inside. He is truly a kind, sensitive, caring young man who has never lost sight of his values or his faith in God. As Brett would say, "He is truly my best friend. He is the one person I can call with a problem, and I know he will be there for me, and he will keep everything confidential." When Brett had his knee surgery last year, Rocky took off after practice to come and stay with him. A few weeks later, he knew Brett would not be able to play ball for a while, so he called and made arrangements for Brett to go watch him in the Big XII Championship. Rocky has always been there for his friends, and despite all his fame and glory, he still just wants to be Rock.

Many will say, "And who *is* Rock?" Rock is a kid at heart. Rocky is the one who always wants to play, whether it's wrestling, tearing around the house, or "accidentally" aiming for Papa with a BB gun and hitting him. Rocky loves to have fun; he laughs, teases, pesters, and pokes at you, and he's always busy.

We could tell stories all day long about Rocky and sports, but despite all of the fame and glory, Rocky has stayed true to his values, his friends, his family, and, most of all, his God—and that is Rocky's true story. Rocky knows he has a God-given talent and has never taken it for granted. No one has ever outworked him or taken his role more seriously. And Rocky is truly more than just a football player. He has used his talents and abilities as a witness to others and as a role model to young people. He is a sensitive, caring young man, and a child at heart. He has been and always will be my third son and Brett's best friend.

Friend and coach, David Rosenthal

I went to high school with Kathy Johnson and met her husband Jim Butler when we were in college. I was in their wedding; Jim and I had a lot in common regarding the football scene.

I was a college player at Oklahoma State, and he was at Tulsa University. We lost touch for a few years but came back together when our son Todd and his son Brett began playing football at Jenks. Brett happened to be best friends with Rocky Calmus, and we met "the Rock" through that relationship.

Jim Butler was the head football coach of one of the two Jenks football teams Rocky's sixth grade year. I was his assistant coach and called a lot of the plays from the booth.

Our big rivals that year were the other Jenks team and the Owasso Rams. The Rams were a well-organized team with a lot of confidence, and they posed as a real threat to knocking off the previous year fifth grade state champions—Jenks. We had an away game that was really going to test us. So off we went up Highway 169 to Owasso, which is about fifteen miles north of Tulsa.

It was customary to have a weigh-in around an hour before the game. If a player weighed over 125 pounds, he couldn't be a running back. He had to put a stripe on his helmet, which designated to the referees that this player could not run with the ball or catch a pass and run with the ball. In addition, there were two- and three-stripers who had to play with other restrictions. This rule was put into play to help prevent injuries.

Rocky, 7th Grade

Rocky was always tall for his age and usually pushed the limits for a running back. The scales to weigh the players were up to the home team, and there could be some variation from one scale to another. Thus, you never knew what kind of scale you would get. Well, to our dismay Rock weighed in at 127 pounds! The Owasso coaches emphatically told us he could not be a running back. Jim Butler went into a courtroom defense lawyer act, and when he was through, even I thought 127 was the same as 125. I think he invented a new kind of math!

However, the Owasso coaches weren't convinced. Jim looked at me and started walking away. I knew from his look that I was to follow. Once we were around the corner, he asked me if I could get two pounds off Rock in the next thirty minutes. I told him I could, but I wanted an okay from Myrle, Rock's dad. We both agreed that his mother, Linda, should be kept away. I took Rock to my car in just his underwear, wrapped a blanket around him, and turned the heater on high. In addition, I gave him a cup to spit in while we began the sweating process. I stayed in the car with him, making sure he was okay and talking to him about life in general. I had to get out of the car twice and towel off myself. If I had not had such a receding hairline, I might have qualified as a running back myself after this ordeal! But after thirty minutes, we took Rocky out, toweled him off, and continued to have him spit in the cup as we walked to the weighing scales once again.

I remember one of their coaches, a guy named Gibbs. He was a real stickler for the rules. Jim told them we wanted to weigh Rocky one more time before the game started. He looked at us and said, "Okay," very confidently. Then Rock stood up and tipped the scales at 124¾ pounds. *Bingo*! If I had a camera, I would have taken a picture of Coach Gibbs' face! He had some reading glasses on, and he looked at us over the top of the glasses with this puzzled look and said, "How did you do that?"

That is not the whole story. We had a couple of candy bars and Gatorade waiting, and old Rock probably gained five pounds—in fifteen minutes.

They kicked off to us and we went down the field and scored on several key runs made by Rocky. We made our extra point and led 7-0. When Rocky came off the field from the extra point, he just fell on his face on our sideline. We got some fluids in him during the second quarter, but Owasso scored during that quarter to bring the score to 7-6. They missed the extra point, so the score was 7-6 at halftime. Once we got the fluids back in Rocky, he committed to playing defense the rest of the game and not offense. After making half of our tackles in the second half, the Trojans won 7-6 and drove south down Highway 169 once again—to the amazement of the Rams.

We met Owasso in the playoffs and defeated them 6-0 in the championship game later that year. The only touchdown in that game was by a sleek running back that weighed in at 124 ¾ pounds—named Rocky Calmus.

Friend, Brooke Barnes

Rocky has always been a role model to the people around him. I've known Rocky for close to nine years, and he's always been such a great friend and special person to my family. He's like a big friendly teddy bear! I'll never forget how we used to fight like brother and sister when we were younger; I was dating his best friend, and he was dating my best friend. I'm so proud of Rocky and all of his outstanding accomplishments! It has truly been an honor to watch him win two

Brooke Barnes and Rocky

state championships in high school and a national championship in college.

One memory from our sophomore year at OU that I never forget was when Rocky, Teri, and I all had a class together, and Rock had a cast on his right hand. We were getting ready to take a test, and I was sitting on the right side of Rocky with Teri on his left when he decided he wanted his cast off. So he just starts ripping it off and went and got scissors so he could cut it the rest of the way off. The smell was enough to knock you out, and of course, I just happened to be sitting on that side of him. Rock thought it was hilarious and kept putting his hand in my face; I gagged my way through the exam.

Brooke, Rocky, and girlfriend Teri

Rocky is an extremely talented young man who has already accomplished a lot in his lifetime, and I'm sure will achieve so much more!

Friends, Jim and Retha Barnes

We have known Rock since 1993, when we moved back to Tulsa from the Edmond/Oklahoma City area. Rocky was Brett Butler's best friend, and Brett was our daughter's first boyfriend when she was in the eighth grade. Rocky and Brett played football for the Jenks Central and Jenks East football teams, respectively. Our daughter, Brooke, was a cheerleader at Jenks East.

Rocky caught our attention the first time we met him. His personality and leadership qualities have always been prominent, in addition to his awesome athletic ability. Rock leads by example—i.e., through hard work, determination, dedication, toughness, high moral standards, compassion, and passion. Rocky's character is his most important feature. He is the same today as he was yesterday, and he will be the same tomorrow and in the future. Rock's status as a Jenks and OU football star has not changed him at all. He is still the same high-quality young man we met in the eighth grade.

Rocky played basketball, football, and baseball in the ninth grade at Jenks High School. During basketball season, Rocky was having ankle trouble and was not allowed to play in one of the home games. He still dressed out for the game, though, and sat next to the coach in hopes that he could enter the game. When the game got close, Rocky's competitive nature took over. He kept looking across the court at his mother and motioning that he was going to play. His mother kept mouthing, "No," and Rocky kept getting more animated. He even went to the scorer's table and acted as though he was going to check himself into the game. It killed him that he could not help his team out. So it came as no surprise to us when he played all of one year at OU with a cast on his hand. He has played his entire career with nagging injuries. It takes his mother's "*No*" to keep him out of a game—*ha*!

Our first glimpse of Rocky's athletic prowess came in an eighth grade football game between Jenks East and Jenks Central. Both schools were unbeaten and were playing each other in the last game of the year. Many of the boys had played on the same teams together in their younger years, so this game was very important! Rocky carried the Central team to victory, acting like a man among boys! He made most of the tackles and physically dragged the Jenks East team up and down the field when he carried the ball. It took several East players riding his back to bring him down. It is a sight we will never forget! Jenks Central won the game by one touchdown.

Also, we will never forget the 1999 OU vs. Notre Dame game in South Bend. Seven players from Jenks High School played in the game. We got them all together after the game to take pictures and reminisce. In fact, Brooke's boyfriend of five years, Sean Mahan, was the starting offensive guard for Notre Dame and was one of Rocky's old Jenks teammates.

Rock gives 110 percent and leads by example. One of the most notable examples of this occurred in the 1996 state championship game against Midwest City. Rocky was a junior at the time. He rushed for over 220 yards and had twenty-two tackles as well. One of our best friends was the vice president and general of KOTV Channel Six at the time. We asked him to have the sports director make a copy of their unedited footage from the game to give to Rocky for Christmas. This was up-close, sight and sound from ground level footage!

The sports director told us that he had overheard a conversation during the game when one of the Midwest City players was coming off the field. He stopped near the head coach and said, "Coach, that number twenty is *bad*!"—as in tough to tackle and impossible to run against.

Of course, we will never forget the 1997 Jenks team, the best team in Oklahoma high school history. Rocky and his teammates were the best defensive team that we have ever seen at any level of football!

We have many fond memories of Rocky, Brooke, and their friends from the eighth through twelfth grades at Jenks and then later while they were at OU. We went to every football and basketball game, since Brooke was a cheerleader and Rock was our favorite player. Rock often rode home with us after several of the games before the kids were old enough to drive. Rocky,

Brooke, Brett, and Brandi, a cheerleader with Brooke, wanted to go to Sonic or Mazzio's after every game!

When Brooke was on crutches, which happened quite often because of nagging ankle problems, Rocky carried her book bag to class. He has always been the big brother that Brooke never had.

Also, we will never forget Brooke's fifteenth birthday party at the Summit Club in downtown Tulsa. We reserved a room and invited several of Brooke's friends for a fun-filled night on top of the Bank IV tower in downtown Tulsa. When the waiter brought out the entrée, a filet mignon, Rocky turned to one of the girls and whispered, "Is this all we get? I'm hungry! Can I have part of yours as well?" Young boys have big appetites, and Rocky's was *legendary*! It was a wonderful evening that we will cherish forever.

Rock has recently taken up the game of golf. We played together several times this summer. He approaches golf the same way he approaches every other athletic endeavor—with vigor and skill. In fact, I saw him hit several drives that were over three hundred yards! That's up there in Tiger Woods' league!

We continue to call Rock at least once a week during football season to leave a "good luck" voice mail message prior to each game. We also correspond via email on a year-round basis and have done so since Rocky started at OU. We also stay in touch through Brooke, since they had classes together at OU.

We have developed many wonderful memories over the years and hope to continue to do so for a lifetime to come! We love Rock as if he were our own and greatly appreciate Linda and Myrle sharing him with us. Rock has been and always will be very special to us. He is the son we never had, our adopted son.

Rocky and good friend Jim Barnes
Jenks Trojans 6A State Champions Dec. 6, 1996

Brett Butler, Jim Barnes, and Rocky
Showing off 6A State Championship rings

Friend, John D. Johnston

Rocky has been one of my closest friends since we were in ninth grade. Rocky and Teri are together because Rocky and I went to Young Life camp the summer of our sophomore year. We met a lot of friends there and that led to Rocky meeting Teri.

I remember a funny story from when Rocky and I went on a ski trip with my church in the tenth grade. We were in a really small town eating lunch. A lot of us were loitering around a newspaper stand and Rocky was joking around, showing us how you could get a newspaper out of the machine without paying for it. Unknown to Rocky, a plainclothes cop was standing right there. He was one of those small town cops with an attitude.

He started talking about arresting Rocky and made a big deal about the newspaper. Rocky said they were just kidding and offered a quarter for the paper, but the cop would have none of it. He finally let us go—under the charge of the youth director, who then also made a big deal about it. He said Rocky would have to do some church service when we got back. This was just some kids having fun! We thought everyone's reaction to it was crazy. What I really admire about Rocky, however, is that after we got back I told him to forget about doing the work at the church. But Rocky showed up at the church and did the work! That's just the kind of guy he is.

Rocky and John Johnston
Jenks High School State Championship
1997

Rocky is a great role model for kids—and for me. He is someone I want my kids to be like. He has a great attitude, works hard, and has a great relationship with the Lord. He will always sign autographs for kids, even if he really doesn't want to, because he remembers what it was like to be a kid. You just couldn't have a better friend.

John's mother, Kathy Johnston

I fondly remember one afternoon right after Rocky and John had gotten their driver's licenses, Rocky came by looking for John, but he had just left on an errand. Football had bonded them as fast friends and they spent a lot of time together. After discovering that I was making chocolate chip cookies, Rocky decided he would wait for John and help me make cookies. He is an excellent partner in baking cookies and an *expert* at tasting them. I made cookies under Rocky's watchful eye, and John soon returned from his errand. Both boys retired from the kitchen—but not before they had their fill of cookies—and playing John Madden football on Play Station.

John's father, John A. Johnston

I never will forget the eighth grade football game between the two Jenks teams. Rocky was on one team and John was on the other. Of course, Rocky always dominated with his size and skill, but on one particular play, Rocky was doing a sweep around the end that John was covering. With John's speed, he had no trouble catching up with Rocky—but what to do with Rocky once he caught him was a different story. John grabbed Rocky's leg and was holding on for dear life; he did manage to hold on for a while. Rock dragged him until reinforcements came to John's rescue to tackle Rocky.

Brad's Wedding
Rocky(OU), John Johnston (OSU), and Brad Hawkins (TU)

Friend, and Second Cousin Paula Foster

I remember some special quotes. For instance, during the 1996 6A championship game against MidWest City, one of their players said, "That guy is bad, really bad."

I also remember when Jenks coach, Allan Trimble, was asked if Rocky was the best high school player he had seen, that he said that he was "the best he had ever coached."

Thanks, Rocky! You will be long remembered by Jenks and OU fans as a "Great One!"

Family friends, Julie and Jeff Luke

My husband Jeff and I—a.k.a. "Birdie and Bean"—became Rocky's adopted "Norman parents." We fed him, took him to the lake, listened to his war stories, and kept an eye on him for his years in Norman. We also dog-sat with Owen—Rocky and Teri's dog—and tried to be there for Myrle and Linda's "baby."

Rocky really is just a good person. We have had nothing to do with that; he came that way. In fact, we tried to corrupt him but did not succeed! People often ask us how much of an influence we've had over Rock, and in answer, I'd say not much.

Rocky is a genuine person, always nice, and he never says a bad word about anyone. He lived with us at times, and I guess the only bad thing was when we'd go to the fridge to get something and Rock had beaten us to it. Oh, one more bad thing. He always hits me!

Rocky with friends, Julie and Jeff Luke

He's pretty good-looking, except when he wears his cap backwards. He did that when we went to the store together. I walked in front of him and acted as if I didn't know him.

Rocky loves children. He has been to visit us frequently at Lake Texoma. If we were at the beach, the kids would flock around to crawl all over him. Rocky often threw them up in the air and into the water, and they would go back to him again and again.

I have just one unusual memory of Rocky. One year when his birthday came along, I baked him a German chocolate cake, my favorite. Can you believe he doesn't like pecans or coconut? Go figure. I just assumed everybody loves German chocolate cakes.

Kansas State Kinfolk
Kyle, Aunt Muriel Ihde, baby Jordan Plaice, Jennifer Ihde, Uncle Wilbur Ihde

Grandma Elma and grandchildren
Back, left to right: JarredAdams, Mandy Calmus, Dawn Musgrove, John Musgrove, Jamie Adams, Lance Calmus
Front: Richie Calmus, Grandma Elma, and Rocky

CHAPTER EIGHT

Double Tragedies

During Rocky's little league football days, Rocky developed a friendship with Ryan Barnes. The Barnes family loved football, and the dad, Gary, was the wild and crazy football announcer. Rock loved going to their house, which was in an area of more well-to-do folks. One time, Ryan and Rocky went to the state fair, and Gary gave them each twenty dollars. Rock was about nine years old and wasn't used to that much money.

Two of Gary's three sons were killed in a tragic car accident; to say it was devastating is a drastic understatement! Gary asked Rocky to be an honorary pallbearer. He also asked Rock to wear his football jacket. The double funeral was very well attended, expertly prepared, and was a gut-wrenching service. Grown men, not even in the family, shook and sobbed uncontrollably.

The oldest son, Darren, in his dress Navy whites, paid tributes to his brothers; there was not a dry eye in attendance. Local television personalities, politicians, and community leaders spoke of the fine young men and the Barnes family.

After the service, Rocky said to his mother, "Mom, I want to do something for Mr. Barnes. Can I give him my football jacket?"

She responded, "Yes, honey, it is yours, and I think that would be just fine—if that's what you want."

After the graveside rites, in private and without any fanfare, Rocky gave his football jacket to Gary. Gary was touched to say the least, and Linda was very proud of her son.

Gary and Darren have been very good friends, and they will always have a place in the hearts of Rocky and all of the Calmuses. The Barnes family is always on the sidelines of Jenks football games and supports the OU Sooners also.

Gary's Letter: Rocky Gave Me His Jacket

In March 1998, Rocky attended the funeral of Ryan and Greg Barnes. These were my two sons, ages nineteen and twenty-three, who were killed in a traffic accident.

Ryan and Rocky had played little league football together at Jenks. I was also the press box announcer for Rocky and Richie's football games. As a result of my involvement, I came to know Rocky and Richie very well.

At the gravesite following the funeral, Rocky presented me with the personalized Jenks football jacket he had received for being a member of the 1997 Class 6A state champions. I hugged him warmly, and it touched my heart. Needless to say, this was an extremely emotional day for me, but Rocky's generosity was a bright spot.

I will forever cherish that special moment when Rocky displayed such a big heart and caring attitude. I was able to witness firsthand the other side of Rocky Calmus. That thoughtful and gentle side is perhaps under-appreciated.

Boy have I enjoyed wearing that jacket to various public places! With the name "Calmus" emblazoned on the front and the number twenty, I have been the recipient of a lot of comments about Rocky. On several occasions, I was asked if I was Rocky's father! I admit it; one time I answered, "Yes." I just couldn't resist.

Gary Barnes and Rocky

I anticipate I will continue to have a lot of fun with all the attention directed my way when I wear the Calmus jacket. It is one of the dearest gifts I have ever received. I wouldn't part with it for the world. Well, on second thought, if Rocky becomes a big time NFL star I might consider auctioning it off on eBay.

Thank you, Rocky, from the bottom of my heart.

CHAPTER NINE

Coaches' Corner and Comments

There have been great high school coaches at Jenks, a large 6-A school that has won six back-to-back state championships.

Head Coach Allan Trimble once said, "Rocky was the kingpin of the group. Aside from his ability, Calmus has an insatiable appetite for the game. He played with a cracked rib, and sprained knee, a deep thigh bruise, and a separated shoulder. The knot on his leg from the thigh bruise would have kept a lesser player out several weeks. Instead, the week after he was hurt, Calmus carried the ball thirty-six times for 226 yards, scored three touchdowns, and passed for another in the state championship game." "He's a throwback—he's from a different generation," says Trimble, "and he doesn't really need a facemask."

Tag Gross, once a Jenks' offensive coach, is now head football coach at Holland Hall. He was an excellent coach, a very good English teacher, and a good role model as well. Rocky became friends with his young son, who also wore a number twenty jersey. Rocky wanted Coach Tag to attend the Butkus ceremony, and he did—paying for his own airfare, an expensive room, and a tuxedo. Now that's a good friend! Coach Tag has a precious family; Rocky loves and appreciates them. Coach Tag has always been one of Rocky's favorites.

Coach, Tag Gross

I have three very vivid memories of Rocky. The first is in the 1996 State Championship game of his junior year. We were playing Midwest City, and Rocky was our tailback and weak side linebacker; he had suffered a thigh bruise the week before that limited him at tailback a little. In the middle of the second quarter, we hadn't moved the ball at all, and we faced a fourth and three at midfield.

Until this point Rocky hadn't played any tailback. We put him in, and we threw a tailback pass, which he completed, to Brett Butler for a touchdown. At halftime, the score was 17-7 in favor of Midwest City. Rocky had only played that one play in the first half.

It took me some time to get from the press box to the locker room at Lewis Field. When I walked in, Rocky cornered me and let me know that he needed to run the ball. He was very animated and was confident that he would get the job done. Well, he ran the ball thirty-six times in the second half for three touchdowns and 221 yards while playing every down at linebacker. Jenks won 28-17, starting the consecutive State Championship streak under Coach Trimble. When I finally saw Rocky after the game, he apologized for his outburst at halftime. I realized then how special he was. He combined an incredible desire to win with being a tremendously good kid.

My second vivid memory of Rocky was during his sophomore year at OU. My son Cooper is a huge fan of Rocky's and has been since he was two years old. Rocky has a special way with kids and had made an impression on Cooper at an early age, before he knew anything about football or how good Rocky is. Cooper wanted to invite him to his fifth birthday party. We told Rocky, knowing he was very busy at OU. The party was on a Saturday afternoon. I was finishing basketball practice on Friday afternoon when Rocky walked into the gym at Jenks. I was surprised and asked him what he was doing there. He told me he was coming to the birthday party the next day. He came, and all the kids were excited he was there and had pictures taken with him. It made Cooper's day that Rocky took the time and energy to come to his party.

My third memory of Rocky is from quite recently. He was off one weekend and came home to Tulsa. My new school, Holland Hall, was playing a football game on a Saturday night. I spoke to Rocky on Friday and asked him if he would speak to my team. He said yes. I didn't tell the team he was coming, and Rocky showed up forty-five minutes before the game as we were warming up. I was standing in the middle of the field and noticed the young men on my team turning their heads and looking over my shoulder to the sideline. Rocky was standing there. When Rocky walked in to speak to the team, everybody became silent and looked up wide-eyed. He gave a great speech, which I knew was uncomfortable for him, but his presence alone made a huge impact on everybody. I had many people tell me later how gracious he was during the game. Once everybody realized he was there, he was mobbed with fans. He signed autographs all night!

Assistant Coach (running backs) for Jenks High School in 1996, Blair Culley

If you are familiar with the Jenks Trojan football program, you are also familiar with the run of the Calmus boys. And run they have, for over two decades. First came Lance, Richie was next, and then there was Rocky.

My relationship with Rocky began in 1996, his junior year in high school. I learned very early on that Rocky was a quality, respectful, and committed young man of character. I can remember a few times late in a game when Rocky would hesitate going into the game at tailback because he had so much respect for the senior ahead of him that he thought that he should finish the game.

Rocky, 9th grade

Rocky has always been the "yes sir" or "no sir" type of person—that's just the way he operates. I can recall phone calls he has made to me from his cell phone as he is ordering from the drive-through. He will patiently wait for a break in our conversation, ask me to hold, and I'll overhear him apologize for a miscommunication on an order, or politely request an extra drink. But that's just Rocky; he's such a gentleman in a society where we could certainly stand more like him.

He truly believes in the Bible verse that describes how we should consider others better than ourselves. He often represents what being humble is all about. Unlike many individuals of Rocky's stature, he treats everyone equally. If you simply met him on the street, not knowing who he was, you would never know he was a high school and collegiate All-American, a Butkus Award Winner, and debatably the best college football player in the country.

Rocky is a unique individual, and I'm a better person for having had the opportunity to spend time with him.

Some of the highlights of Rocky's Jenks career include the following: he was a two-way starter for three years, starting as both a running back and a line backer. Jenks won the 6A State Championship Rocky's junior and senior years in high school with a record of 39-2. In those two years, he had 128 tackles, fifty-three of which were unassisted, made fifteen tackles causing a loss of yards, and had five quarterback sacks. Rocky rushed 1,268 yards, scored twenty-four touchdowns, blocked three passes, made two fumble recoveries, and only fumbled himself twice.

By the time he was done in high school, he had rushed 2,823 yards, had 388 tackles, and had made forty-nine touchdowns.

Coach Tag Gross and Coach Brent Venables

Rocky was the Most Valuable Player of the 1997 6A State Championship, having rushed for 223 yards and scored five touchdowns. The 1998 6A State Championship against Yukon was so lopsided, it was not televised—but Rocky would have been MVP again.

Rocky won the Jim Thorpe Award, was a Blue Chip player, and was All-State Football, All-District, and All-American. He was also the Defensive Player of the Year in Oklahoma.

CHAPTER TEN

Preachers, Praise, and Defending the Faith

Rocky's fist time at church was when he was approximately one week old. The Calmus kids were raised in church, and though they weren't always sitting on the edge of their seat, they knew they had better act like it. Deciding to "bring children up in the love and admonitions of the Lord" so that they don't depart from it is the most important decision a parent will ever make.

Rocky's faith has been amazing. In this day and age, it is difficult to stand out in a crowd for the right reasons, but God has given him the faith, wisdom, and courage to do just that.

Here are a few good men and women that assisted Rocky along the way, starting with Frank Chase—friend, evangelist, and former hardened criminal from the south side of Tulsa, once imprisoned for life. Frank was gloriously saved and has been serving God since his miracle pardon. He and wife Ramona and children Laura and John attend the Southwest Nazarene church with the Calmus family. Rocky was saved at one of Frank's hell-fire and damnation revival services. They are servants of God, friends, and people who do live what they preach.

Reverend Frank and Ramona Chase

Ramona and I are so proud of you. You were just a big kid when we first got to know you. After we heard how you have taken a public stand for the Lord and your Christian beliefs, I was thrilled to recall that you came to know Jesus and got saved one day under my preaching. Ramona, as your Sunday school teacher in junior high, mostly recalls you sleeping—while sitting up! However, that's okay; she is proud of you too. We love your whole family and are proud to count them not only as church family but also as friends. You are always in our prayers. Keep up the good work, keep the Lord first, and you will continue to excel.

The Calmus' current pastors at Southwest Nazarene are new, but everyone has fallen in love with young Tim, Jeanette, and Chip Cole.

Two things Pastor Tim, a Jayhawks fan, said he would never do: Root for the Sooners and preach in Oklahoma. Guess what! Rock and the whole Sooner team had an attentive fan from Kansas University.

Appreciation Day at Southwest Nazarene

In February 2001, the teen leader at Southwest Nazarene, Malinda Aary, wanted to do something for Rocky because he was so good at doing for others. So, Malinda, Pastor Tim, and the Sunday school planned a special celebration. They made crimson number twenty shirts with "S.W. Nazarene" on the front and "Calmus" on the back. The congregation went wild, and almost everyone in the audience wore one; it was a great sight. All of Rocky's family members spoke, and we had to pull Grandma Pauline Calmus off the stage (not really). We did not advertise, but the usual congregation of 125 people swelled to about 250. When Rocky got to the podium and looked over the ground, he could not speak. He tried several times, and his eyes watered as he thanked the church, his parents, family, and the Lord for his many blessings. Rocky got a standing ovation; it was a very special day.

Special T-shirts made up for Appreciation Day

The Calmus family
Lance, Myrle, Rocky, Linda, Mandy, and Richie

Even with a cast on his writing hand, he signed pictures, shirts, footballs, and took photos for two hours. Thanks to Bill Cooley, the whole thing is on video tape!

Pastor Tim gave an excellent sermon about life, heroes, and the path that God leads us if we allow him. At one point he shared, "Rocky, do not let football be the focus of your life; but allow God to be the focus and football to be the vehicle to share the word to others."

Former pastors and family friends, Mike and Suzanne Murray

The Calmus family attended Southwest Church of the Nazarene in Tulsa, Oklahoma, while my wife and I were pastors there. Myrle, Linda, Lance, Richie, Mandy, and Rocky were a sports family in every sense of the word, and as we grew closer to the Calmuses, we enjoyed their accomplishments along with them.

Rocky and Suzanne Murray

I can remember one evening while having dinner at the Calmus home. Rocky, being the sweet, kind, innocent kid he always has been, started coming by and messing up my hair. I told him to stop, but he kept doing it! When I had enough, I told him that if he did it again, I was going to get him.

He obviously thought I was bluffing or couldn't catch him, and it was only a matter of time until he came by again. This time as he messed up my hair, he ran off—but this time I was right behind him. As he passed through the hallway and the front entry and into the living room, I was close on his heels, and I leaped into the air and tackled him to the floor.

He was very surprised when I held him down! It took all I had, but I kept him down and proved my point. Later, Myrle told me that I was in a very elite group as one of those who have tackled number twenty, the Rock.

Rocky, I want you to know how proud we are of you. As young people look for heroes today, I am proud to point you out to them. You are a very special young man, and you've got limitless potential!

Friend, Cherry Murray

I remember Rocky as the typical little brother. You never wanted him around, but somehow he was always there! The two words that best describe the way I remember him would have to be "pest" and "annoying."

I remember that one summer during Vacation Bible School, I was teaching a class of preschool-aged kids. Rocky came by repeatedly to pester them, and we had to direct him back to his class again and again.

Rocky, you've turned into an incredible young man. Remember that it isn't your athletic skills or intelligence that determines you're success, however—it's your character. And with character as the determining factor, I have no doubt that you will be very successful in life. Congratulations for everything that you've accomplished already, and I wish you the best of luck as you go into the future.

Pastor of Emmaus Baptist Church, Mike Booth

Rocky first came to Emmaus Baptist Church on a Sunday in August of 2000. He came with Teri Marcum, and she had attended the week before with some teammates and had liked the service.

That first Sunday, I was sitting on the front row of the west section. I sit in the pews rather than on the stage, and as I was singing, I caught sight of something out of the corner of my eye—someone entering the auditorium through the west doors. Since these doors are close to the stage, few people enter through them because they don't want to be seen by everyone else in the congregation. I turned in time to see a young man, dressed in a nice T-shirt and shorts. I remember thinking to myself, "That looks like Rocky Calmus."

Since we're in the Moore school district, everyone knows what Rocky Calmus looks like—even before he came to OU—because he played for Jenks, which kept beating Moore in the high school playoff games. I wondered if it really was him, however, because I couldn't imagine why he would come to Emmaus.

After we sang a few songs, we had a welcome time to greet people. He had sat a few rows behind me, and I worked my way back to shake his hand and introduce myself.

"I'm Mike Booth," I told him.

"I'm Rocky Calmus," he replied politely.

"Yes, I know. I know you," I told him. "But you don't know me! That's why I'm introducing myself."

The whole time I was preaching, I wondered what Rocky Calmus was doing in one of our services.

A couple of weeks later, I went to one of Teri's soccer games. OU was playing the University of Texas. That Sunday afternoon was windy, wet, and cool, but I felt obliged to be there because many of the team members had been coming to Emmaus. Rocky also came, and people began to swarm around him. He signed autographs and talked to spectators while trying to see Teri play.

The girls managed to rally in the last three minutes and beat Texas, and after the game I went to congratulate the girls I knew from church. I found Teri removing the tape from her socks with Rocky right behind her. I complimented her on the game, and she was very thankful that I had come to watch and then asked when the evening service was. I told her, and she responded that she'd be there. Quickly I looked up at Rocky and asked, "Are you coming too?"

His reply was fantastic. He said, "I go where she goes."

They both came to the service and I introduced Teri to the congregation as one of the girls on OU's soccer team. I announced their win over Texas and said, "You may want to shake her hand and meet her boyfriend, Rocky Calmus." That was the first time many in the church heard that Rocky and Teri were attending Emmaus, and after the service, we went out to eat together to celebrate the victory over Texas.

A few weeks later, *Sports Illustrated* did an interview with Rocky and published his story. In it, he mentioned that he attended Oklahoma City's Emmaus Baptist Church. One of our college students, a big OU fan, called our college minister, Jeron Young, and told him that we were in *Sports Illustrated*. Thinking that the student was talking about the football team, Jeron was only somewhat excited—it had been a long time since OU had gotten any good press from *S.I.* However, when he learned that Rocky had mentioned our church specifically, Jeron burst into my office to inform me. I was astonished to say the least!

God used all that in a wonderful way. David, a young man in our church, is suffering from a reoccurring brain tumor. He is in his thirties, has a wife and five children, and is a big OU fan. I explained his situation to Rocky and Teri, and I asked them if they would go with me to David's house to autograph a copy of *Sports Illustrated*. They met me at the church, and I took them to David's house, where they signed the magazine and a photo. Before we left, we prayed for David and his family. Rocky showed his true character in sacrificing an evening during the season to help brighten someone's day.

Every March, Emmaus has a youth weekend we call "Impact." Since we had so many OU athletes attending the church, we decided to ask them to be teachers and group leaders for the weekend. I asked Rocky and Teri if they would be keynote speakers at the Saturday night service. The theme of the weekend was moral purity, and I wanted to interview them about their dating relationship. I finally got them to agree, and the service was great—our youth were challenged to remain pure until marriage through Rocky and Teri's testimony.

My wife and I took Rocky and Teri out to eat before the youth weekend's Saturday evening service. We went to one of our favorite restaurants, Zio's. We watched the OU basketball team on TV while we waited to be seated, and during that time, a number of people also waiting noticed Rocky and came over. He listened to them and signed a few autographs.

When they left, I asked if he ever got tired of being recognized wherever he went. He said something to the effect that he knew it wouldn't last forever and that he was just enjoying it while it lasted.

After we were seated, we sat Rocky facing the wall so that nobody would bother him. As we got situated, the women at the table next to us began to whisper to one another; someone else had recognized Rocky. After we ordered our meals, one of the girls got up and approached our table.

"Excuse me," she began, "but aren't you—" As she began talking, I watched Rocky to see his expression as yet *another* fan asked for an autograph. But she continued with "—the guy that spoke at the Baptist Collegiate Ministry in Weatherford a couple of weeks ago?"

She had recognized *me*, not Rocky! We all began to laugh. Apparently, she was attempting to prove to her friends that I was the one, and she had worked up the nerve to ask.

I told her she was right and then pointed to Rocky. "Do you know who this is?" I asked her.

"No," she replied.

"This is Rocky Calmus, from the OU football team."

She shrugged. "I'm an OSU fan," she admitted.

"You should know him then, because he's the one who tackled Aso Pogi!" Rocky had tackled the OSU quarterback for a safety during the Bedlam game.

After she left, I bragged to Rocky that he wasn't the only famous one in the group.

One learns to anticipate pranks with any youth event, and that Sunday, my wife Freddi was leaving the house at 6:00 in the morning. As she opened the front door, a garbage can that had been leaning on the door fell on her, smearing her thoroughly. After further investigation, we found that our cars had also been targeted: the windshields, door, and trunk locks were smeared with Vaseline, and the cars themselves were wrapped with cellophane and had the side mirrors duct-taped. Someone had stuffed hot dog wienies under the door latches. Let me tell you, it's a wonderful feeling when your fingernails sink deep into them!

A For Sale sign was in the front yard, but to top it off, a big cement boulder and goldfish adorned the front porch.

At that point all I was really concerned with was getting Freddi off to work, but later when I found Ryan Fisher, a defensive tackle on the National Championship-winning 2000 team, I blamed him. He denied being involved and said that he had gone home early, sick, the night before.

I didn't really think that Rocky had anything to do with the prank, but as we were returning from church that evening, my wife and I nearly stumbled over the cement block on the porch. Freddi asked me, "When are you going to get rid of this rock?"

At that moment, we both simultaneously thought, "A rock and a fish—Rocky and Fisher!" They had left the signature of their Saturday night's work! We had been pranked by a couple of national champions and a—at the time—Butkus Award Finalist—later the Butkus Award Winner. Of course, they hadn't been alone—they had some female accomplices who had contributed to the exterior decoration of our home.

One of the stories that best represents Rocky's character is the way that he handled his selection for Playboy's Preseason All-American team. He didn't have to pray about it, seek counsel, or spend time thinking—he just turned them down. He was not attempting to be pious or preachy, but he didn't want his picture and name associated with a magazine like that.

The day after he turned them down, we were eating lunch together and studying the first chapter of 1 John. Rocky asked me what I thought of his decision, and I responded by letting him know I supported him and was very pleased by his choice. He was living out his beliefs, and since many young boys in Oklahoma look up to him, he had proved that he was worthy of the responsibility of being a positive role model.

Since that first time Rocky came to Emmaus, I have had the pleasure of getting to know the real Rocky Calmus. Everyone knows he's a great football player, but only a select few get the privilege of getting to know him as anything other than a football star.

Rocky's favorite Bible verse is Philippians 4:13, which says, "I can do all things through Christ who strengthens me." He certainly has used that verse to motivate himself to be the best football player he can be. But I have seen him apply those words to his life, to being the person God wants him to be. Rocky Calmus is an excellent football player, role model, leader, and friend. I pray God's best for him in every way.

Advertising manager of the Baptist Messenger, Jerry Pierce—Sooner Defenders Defending The Faith

As a highly touted linebacker at Class 6A Jenks High School in 1997, Rocky Calmus had his choice of colleges. During a recruiting visit to a prospective campus, a star linebacker assigned to escort Calmus on his weekend trip told him, "You know, there's not an All-American linebacker who doesn't party or drink."

Calmus, an All-American linebacker himself for the top - ranked University of Oklahoma Sooners, has smashed that theory like he does helpless quarterbacks.

"You know," Calmus said, "I don't get why he said that. I'd like to go back to him now and say, 'You know, you're wrong.' That guy is in the NFL now. He's successful. But it's sort of like saying you're not going to be successful unless you go out and party and hang out with the guys."

Calmus, unlike the oft-cast stereotype of a big-time college athlete, prefers his Baptist church to college-town parties.

Calmus and teammate Ryan Fisher, an All-Big XII defensive lineman, are two of about a dozen OU athletes—mainly wrestlers and women's soccer players—who attend Emmaus Baptist Church near Oklahoma City, about ten miles from the OU campus.

Calmus and Fisher rarely miss Sunday morning services. After defeating Kansas State 27-24 in the Big XII Conference Championship on December 2, the team arrived home from Kansas City at 2:45 in the morning. After a couple of hours sleep, Calmus and Fisher hauled their battered bodies to church.

"It's kind of a commitment I made to myself," said Fisher, a big senior, "that no matter winning or losing, I was going to come to church. It wouldn't be right to come sometimes, and then all of the sudden you have a big victory and you're like, 'Ah, I'm just not going to go tomorrow.' I made that commitment to myself before the season began." Calmus, who was one of three finalists for the Butkus Award—given to the nation's top linebacker—said, "Come to church when you're feeling good. Come when life's going right instead of when it's going wrong."

In the late 1980s, OU's football program began a downward spiral that was precipitated by a slew of criminal charges ranging from drug trafficking to gang rape against a handful of players. Fairly or unfairly, OU was portrayed as an outlaw program, NCAA probation followed, as have four head coaches since then. Back then, Calmus and Fisher might have walked a lonely road, but OU football has started intently marching lockstep with Jesus.

The Sooners are "Back on Top," as *Sports Illustrated's* cover proclaimed on November 3, 2000, after they manhandled then-number one Nebraska 31-14. They are winning like the old Sooners, but this team's persona differs from that of twelve or fifteen years ago. Team chapel is in vogue, and fur coats, earrings, gaudy jewelry, and carry-alls are not.

With visible Christians such as Calmus, Fisher, Woolfork, Burcham, Norman, William, and All-American quarterback Josh Heupel leading the charge, OU vied for a seventh national title

January 3, 2000 against the Florida State Seminoles in the Orange Bowl, which they won!

"I think it helps to see people like Rocky and Josh be so successful," Fisher said. "You know, maybe it's different from a few years ago when everybody thought they had to be kinda crazy and have no rules to be successful."

Calmus added, "[Christians] are kind of, like, coming out of the closet.... I guess they aren't afraid to stand up."

Fisher said that team chapel twenty minutes before game time is packed with players and, increasingly, coaches.

"Even guys that maybe go out and stuff, they're there," Calmus said. "It's good to see them. They're saying 'Hey, I'm gonna take the time to go.'"

OU's team chaplain, Mike Whitson, a member of Norman, Bethel, and assistant state director of the Fellowship of Christian Athletes, said the Sooners have always had committed believers in their ranks, but 2000's squad has many more visible Christians.

Coach Bob Stoops and Rocky

Whitson said players such as center Bubba Burcham, slot back Josh Norman, receivers Andre Woolfolk and Elijah Steenhoek, safety Roy Williams, and offensive linemen Scott Kempenich and Howard Duncan, are also spiritual leaders on the team. "I could go on and on," Whitson said. "Coach [Bob] Stoops and his staff do a phenomenal job of holding these kids accountable on and off the field," he added. "We get to play a part in that as well.... It's a tough world they walk into with everybody patting them on the back and telling them how great they are."

Fisher, who grew up in Arlington, Texas, accepted Christ in junior high school through the witness of a family friend that Fisher considers his mentor. He also credits his girlfriend, Courtney Pertree, who also attends Emmaus, and her family, as positive influences in his life.

Calmus said he was saved in middle school during a revival at Southwest Nazarene, which he attended with his family. "Throughout my life, I've gotten off track. But when I met Terri," his high school sweetheart and OU soccer player, "really [over] the last three years, I've gotten stronger beliefs," Calmus said.

Growth came through adversity, Fisher and Calmus admitted. Over the past three seasons, Calmus has at times played with a fractured leg, wrist, and thumb. Yet, he excelled with a team-best 122 tackles, twelve of which were for losses. He snagged an interception for a touchdown against rival Texas while wearing a cast on his wrist and forearm.

"I probably wouldn't be able to do half the things I do [without the Lord], because I'm always injured." Calmus said. "There's no way I could do it, because I'm always hurt. I need something to help me through. It's not my willpower."

CHAPTER ELEVEN

True Love Waits

Associate Editor of the Baptist Messenger, Dana Williamson

Their relationship got off to a "rocky" start. She didn't like him too much, and he admits the first thing that attracted him to her was her "cute little athletic body." But over the past five years, God has worked in the relationship of Rocky Calmus and Teri Marcum. Today, they are committed to God, to each other, and to remaining sexually pure until marriage.

Rocky Calmus is known to Oklahoma and the nation as an All-American linebacker for the national championship-winning University of Oklahoma football team. And not to be downplayed, Teri Marcum is his girlfriend of five years and an OU soccer player who transferred from Oklahoma State University to be closer to Calmus. Marcum was awarded a scholarship to attend OSU after gaining All-American honors as captain of her soccer team at Jenks High School, where both Marcum and Calmus graduated.

Teri said she wanted Calmus to attend OSU also, because OU's football fortunes were at a low when he signed with the Sooners. "However, now I know he made the right decision," said Marcum.

The two athletes met the summer before their junior year at Jenks. They say their relationship has had its ups and downs, but that over the last couple of years they have "regained their spiritual life." Speaking at Youth Impact Weekend at Oklahoma City's Emmaus Baptist Church, where the couple attends services, they said church has helped them remain focused on the truth.

Teri and Rocky

Both grew up in Christian homes. Rocky, a finalist for the coveted Butkus Award, which is given to the nation's top linebacker, said he became a Christian as a seventh grader when his mother dragged him to a revival meeting. "I literally got the hell scared out of me," Calmus said. Teri said she was a mature child and understood who God was. She accepted Jesus, she said, when her mother talked to her and her sister about salvation.

Both Rocky and Teri have favorite Bible verses. Rocky said his is Philippians 4:13: "I can do all things through Christ who strengthens me." Rocky admitted that he initially "used that mostly for sports reasons, but it has come to mean much more than that to me." Teri claims Matthew 6:33 as her verse. It reads, "Seek ye first the kingdom of God, and His righteousness, and all these things shall be added unto you."

Rocky and Teri have been attending Emmaus for more than a year, and although they have not yet joined as members, they said it is their church home. They said going to movies and eating out take up some of their dating time, but most of it is spent in church activities.

Although they say they don't know what God has planned for them as far as marriage goes, the church plays a role in their commitment to moral purity.

"Having God's truth continually instilled into you helps in that area," said Teri. "Church is a place where you can remain focused on the truth and what God wants you to do."

Rocky said he saw the consequences of sexual impurity among friends and acquaintances while he was in high school. "I learned there are emotional and spiritual consequences, as well as physical," he said. "I want to give my bride something no one else has given her. It will be a special time."

Rocky and Teri at the 2001 Butkus Awards

Rocky

CHAPTER TWELVE

Recruiting Wars

It was fun at first—the letters and the calls, then more calls, then, "It's your turn to answer the phone," to which someone would respond, "Why me?" or, "No, I took the last one; it's your turn."

Big schools, little schools, East Coast, West Coast, Division One, Two, and Juco—they all wrote, called, and hawked their wares. Day and night, night and day, mealtime, bedtime—it seemed there was no end. But finally the Final Four emerged—OU, OSU, K-State, and Ohio State.

There are lots of rules involved in the recruitment procedure, but it mostly pertains to the visits of head coaches. And while there is a dead period, it isn't nearly long enough. Coaches make recruiting trips where they wine, dine, brag, promise, and inflate the truth—whatever it takes to get top athletes to their prestigious schools.

A typical trip for Rocky and his family went something like this: The trip typically started on a Friday with a welcome dinner and a night in a nice hotel, and they were carted around here and there with a schedule in hand.

Rocky
Photo by Jana Monlapig

On Saturday, they began with breakfast, a tour of the campus, and then meetings with the academic advisors. The Calmuses then often toured the football offices and the locker rooms—where they would have a jersey with the young man's name on it, which is impressive the first time but then becomes commonplace. Later in the day, they often toured the cafeterias and the dorms while listening to the proposed career paths for the student, the different areas of help available, and the necessary GPAs for participation—everything.

Saturday evening, the prospective player would go out with his host athlete, who is given money for entertaining the recruit—some actually spend the money on their recruit, but a few actually pocket it for themselves. That evening, Rocky's parents would try to relax.

On Sunday morning, the real "offer wars" would begin. A coach talked with the whole family, and then would usually want to talk to Rocky alone. Linda often felt as though she were dealing with used car salesmen—we can give you this, but we need an answer today; we only have one scholarship left, but it might be gone in a week, etc.

On the recruiting visit to OU, Coach Ryan wanted to go to breakfast at Shoney's alone with the Calmus's instead of the usual vying for their time along with everyone else. That was fine, and Rocky had some burning questions. They talked "46 Defense." Rocky really liked Coach Ryan.

As they ate, the Calmuses noticed two couples in the back of the restaurant. One man had an OU baseball jacket, the other an OU hat. One of the gentlemen came by the table. He walked with a cane and had a moustache.

He said to Rock, "You are Rocky Calmus, aren't you?" This was the first time Rock had been recognized outside the Jenks and Tulsa area. He went on to say that he had followed Rocky's career and that he was a heck of a player. "Young man, we sure need you at OU. I hope you come help us, but if you don't, then I wish you the best of luck." By this time Rocky was grinning from ear to ear. The man said, "I'm a season ticket holder sitting in the south end zone."

Coach Ryan jokingly said, "That was worth the money." The gentleman was very impressive, and no one is sure how much impact such conversations had on Rocky's decision to play for OU.

To that Sooner fan:

A note to you is long overdue, but while reflecting on this book, I thought of you—this unknown fan.

I wanted to thank you for being so polite and knowledgeable about Rocky's football career. You were very encouraging as you told Rocky that OU really needed him. When you acknowledged Rocky, it was the first time he had been recognized outside of the general Tulsa area, and your enthusiasm for Rocky was contagious.

What impressed me the most, however, was that unlike some fanatic fans, you wished him the best of luck in whatever course he decided. Your attitude made my eyes tear up with loving pride, and it made a big impression on Rocky, also—in fact, we don't really know how much impact that might have had on his decision.

Thank you, devoted Sooner fan!

Fondly,

Linda Calmus

The coach that called the most, visited the school and the Calmuses most frequently, even contacted Rocky's girlfriend, and never gave up was Les Miles. At that time, he was offensive coordinator at OSU. He was so animated, so personable, and oh so persistent. On one day there was a good old Oklahoma snowstorm, and somehow Coach Miles tracked Rocky's mom Linda down on her way home from Muskogee. They met at McDonald's—don't worry, NCAA, she bought her own coke. He once again told her how wonderful OSU was, but finally, as it was getting late, she said, "Coach, I've got to go," and left. The trip home was treacherous as she inched along at 10-20 mph, occasionally catching sight of many cars in the ditches. She was not saying nice things about Coach Miles, while gripping the steering wheel with white knuckles. Linda still thinks of Coach Miles as a fun, personable, family man—and a good recruiter. The Calmus family wishes him well in his position as head coach for OSU.

Rocky thought about going to OSU because of his girlfriend Teri. She had a soccer scholarship there. His family told him that if he really wanted to be a Cowboy, that was one thing, but he shouldn't go there because of a high school girlfriend.

OU's defensive Coach, Rex Ryan, as well as his twin brother, defensive OSU Coach, Rob Ryan, were a hoot. They even sounded alike on the phone! Rocky really liked Rex, and he was one of the first to say repeatedly, "Rocky, you are the Defensive Player of the Year in Oklahoma, not in Kansas or

Ohio." Linda made the mistake of serving Rex her famous, made-from-scratch chocolate pie. Word got around quickly, and she had to make a lot of pies. As the "Recruiting Wars" progressed, however, the restaurant Tippins served tasty pies to a lot of coaches.

Coach Simmons was first. He was a knowledgeable, sincere, and soft-spoken man. He was as excited as his demeanor would allow him to have Rocky as a prospect. His wife, Linda, was an RN like Linda Calmus, and they shared some warm fuzzy feelings. Coach Simmons and his wife were lovely people and had a very nice reception in their home for the prospective players and parents.

Coach Rex Ryan and Rocky
Photo by Lisa Hall

Coaches Rex Ryan and Sam Pittman were young, energetic, and pumped up about OU football. They were contagious in their enthusiasm.

One of the coaches that had the greatest impact was not even a football coach but was instead an OU baseball coach,

Larry Coshell. He was a classy, upstanding, wonderful man. He made the trip down the turnpike and really gave Rocky and family some good advice.

He said, "Rocky, do you want to be an alumni from K-State? Are you going to live and work in Manhattan?" Coshell added, "Do not pick a university because of the coach, because they are here today and gone tomorrow. Make sure you really *want* to be there—how close to home are you, what academics do they offer, the facility, the reputation, the tradition." Coach Coshell offered to give Rocky the chance to play baseball also.

Coach Holiday from OSU also visited the Calmus home. He had missed out on their older son, Lance, in the recruiting process, and he did not want to repeat that error. He talked about his son Matt and Rocky becoming roommates, since they had met at All-State and the awards banquet.

Coach Synder and Coach Peterson came to the Calmus home and spent about four hours, very late on a school evening. Rocky's family was getting a little aggravated because Rocky needed to be in bed—plus they'd heard enough. Synder is a workaholic, but he has turned K-State around and is a smart man.

The day Coach Blake from OU was to come to the Calmus house, Coach Peterson from K-State showed up at Rocky's school and convinced him that he should cancel Coach Blake's visit. Time was getting short, and apparently K-State felt that the last horse in the barn would get the most oats.

Rocky called his dad from school and asked Myrle to call Blake to cancel the visit—Peterson was, of course, right there beside him. Mild-mannered, slow-moving, low-key Myrle got his dander up. In about three minutes he arrived at the school and told Coach Peterson, "We listened to you and your coach, and we're listening to Coach Blake."

Linda heard about this when Myrle called, though she didn't know the outcome. However, on the drive home, she heard on one of the radio sports talk shows that Rocky had verbally committed to K-State! She started crying and pulled off the road, and after praying, she drove home like a madwoman. Of course, that rumor wasn't true, and neither were an assortment of others—including the ones that were said to be the "gospel truth."

The OU head coach did make a visit that evening. Coach Blake sat on the couch, and he was the most down-to-earth, personable man. At one point, he said, "After I leave here, I'll cross the river to Sand Springs, and no matter what time it is, my mama will fix me a fried chicken dinner."

Rocky and his dad, Myrle

They talked more about family, Christian values, and the important things in life. He told Rocky that he needed him, he'd have an opportunity to play right away, and that he could help rebuild the program at OU.

It was a very difficult decision for Rocky—one of his high school coaches wanted him to go to K-State, but most coaches and teachers were pushing him to go to OSU. His girlfriend wanted him with her at OSU. OU's football program was down, but Rocky's parents really wanted him to go there, though neither of them had attended OU—in fact, Myrle played baseball for OSU. Rocky had always wanted to be a Sooner, but it looked like all support was for OSU.

Rocky's mom, Linda, spent a lot of time praying. "Lord, please direct Rocky to where You want him. Don't let outside pressures influence him, and help us accept whatever decision he makes." Rocky, of course, was praying almost the same prayer.

#1 God —#1 Sooners!
Rocky

Rocky didn't tell anyone that he chose OU until the very last moment. The day he announced he was heading to OU was a very exciting one for the Calmus family—there were lots of people, cameras, and reporters clamoring to inform the world that Rocky had picked OU. His parents were ecstatic, though in truth there was relatively little support for Rock's choice. Some people were very disappointed, with one woman even telling Linda that Rocky was making a big mistake; even one of Rock's closest friends had negative things to say. After Rock's success—and OU's—the Calmuses wonder what those pessimists are saying now.

The Calmus family thanks God for placing Rocky at OU and for taking the team from near the bottom to be national champions!

The following are two recruiting letters. The first is disgusting, and the second one is hilarious.

Dear Rocky Calmus:

You have made a big mistake going to that looser school. I can't understand why you would go there. OSU is winning; we are going to a bowl game. OU is a loser—and you will be sorry!

Urgent Message to Rocky Calmus:

I wanted to tell you one last time just how important it is that you sign with the University of Oklahoma and stay away from Silo Tech in Stillwater. The Sooners have won six national championships and produced dozens of All-Americans, have had three running backs win the Heisman Trophy, and have a long and glorious football tradition dating back to 1950.

Consider OSU. They only occasionally have a good team and produce a winning record. In their entire football history, they have never demonstrated an ability to sustain any momentum or create a winning legacy. Their prospects for next season are already starting to look pretty slim. All the published reports indicate that the Sooners are definitely having a better recruiting season than the Cowboys.

Rocky
Photo by Jana Monlapig

Rocky, if you were raised a Sooner fan, then how can you consider signing with OSU? Don't you realize that once a Sooner fan, always a Sooner fan? Only our goofy President, Bill Clinton, could be so dishonest as to switch sides and change loyalties. We all know the Norman campus is the center of the football universe in

Oklahoma. Stillwater is an afterthought. OU is coming back and will regain its lofty status in the world of college football. Where has OSU been, and where are they going? Unquestionably, if there is a tradition of winning excellence in our proud state, then it is with the football gods at Owen Field. The Sooners consistently draw crowds around seventy thousand and I've seen crowds at OSU that were not much larger than for a Jenks High School game.

Rocky

You are a rare talent and an exceptional young man. Wherever you choose to play, you will elevate that program and be an inspirational asset. But for true greatness, it takes an entire program—not just one player. In my opinion, OSU does not have the total package and never will. OU has had it and lost it, but they will get it back.

The idea of you playing football for the Sooners is totally awesome; wouldn't you be excited running down the ramp of the Cotton Bowl for the Texas game!? There is no doubt that your talents would be fully utilized in Norman. But in Stillwater, I'm not so sure. I want the entire nation to enjoy watching the stud from Jenks on national TV. You are the most popular athlete to ever graduate from Jenks, and I would be personally thrilled to watch you showcase your skills in the crimson and cream colors of the University of Oklahoma. It would be Jerrod Reese at quarterback, Seth Littrell at fullback, and Rocky Calmus at tailback. It can happen—three homegrown boys using their talents to bring OU out of the football wilderness.

Why would you want to compete with Matt Holiday for publicity in Stillwater either in baseball or football? Go to Norman and be the big kid on the block! A Trojan should not take a back seat to a Pioneer. One final thought: down deep in your heart, don't you truly believe that your devoted fans would rather see you sign with OU? Not just me, but literally hundreds and maybe thousands of us would. OSU is for losers, farmers, and veterinarians. You definitely deserve better.

Thank you for your serious consideration.

Your Devoted Fan

P.S. Also, remember if you sign with the Aggies, you will never hear me yell *Rocko* again. I'm Sooner born and Sooner bred, and when I die, I'll be Sooner dead. I can never, ever cheer for you again if you play football with the FFA crowd in Stillwater. I will also be forced to admit that I secretly admire Richie more than you. But as a consolation prize, should you become a dorky Cowboy, I will buy you a John Deere cap, a plug of chewing tobacco, and a lifetime supply of animal tranquilizers.

CHAPTER THIRTEEN

Beginning a Rocky Road at OU

That first year, OU had a losing season, but seventy thousand fans still showed up bleeding crimson and cream.

Rocky's first summer was difficult but fun. His first summer job was working at a beer company. His mother and father did not like that, so they called Merv Johnson and asked him to find Rocky something else. Rocky made two fewer dollars an hour, but he had a higher paying job in Tulsa on Fridays that more than made up for it. God does give favor to the faithful!

Myrle and Linda missed Rocky's first start in college because Richie was in his senior year at Southeastern, playing as a tailback. The Savages were not as prestigious as the Sooners, but Richie could zigzag down the field with the best of them.

Rocky thought he'd be a sophomore when he got his first chance to start, but the coaches thought he was ready and started him at strong side linebacker in the Missouri game on October 18, 1998. In that first game, he had eight tackles, blocked an extra point attempt, and also blocked a punt. Though the defense played well, OU didn't take home a win that night, however.

Rocky's second game as a starter was the bedlam game against OSU, where his girlfriend Teri attended, along with some of Rock's Jenks friends. Rocky and his friend John Johnston e-mailed "smack" to each other all week. OU lost, 41-26, and it was one of the most difficult losses of Rocky's college career.

Rocky

Coach Rex Ryan had nothing but praise for Rocky. "He's the Oklahoma Defensive player of the year, so you know he's going to be some kind of player…. He goes one hundred percent." Ryan did qualify Rocky's playing as a freshman by saying, "He might not always do the right thing because he's still learning, but he's playing hard and aggressive. That's what you want as a coach. That's all you can ask." Rocky loved playing for Coach Ryan and would love to do it again—perhaps in the NFL one day.

Things seemed to go downhill from there following multiple changes and new schemes—but nothing seemed to work. Rock was not used to losing; in fact, he only lost three times in his entire career prior to going to OU. In his first year, he'd lost seven games. It was tough, really tough, but Rocky still believed and had faith. In a newspaper article in late October, he said, "It's going to turn around—at least that's what I'm expecting. People say history repeats itself, and I think it should in the next three years. It's a winning tradition."

Nineteen ninety-eight was not all bad. Rocky was one of the Top Freshmen Twelve Conference, was Second Year

Freshman All-Big XII, and was fifth in the league in tackles—making fifty-five in the year, thirty of which were unassisted. He made eleven tackles for loss, which was good enough to make him third best in squad and sixteenth in the Big XII. He averaged 7.8 tackles per game as a starter.

Rocky's high school buddies
Freddi, Chase, Rocky, Brett, and Jimmy

The most impressive start his freshman year was a 4.0 grade average! Myrle and Linda had to be resuscitated after they heard that news.

Rocky was awarded the Jay Myers Award, which is given to a true freshman for excellence in his or her chosen athletic field while maintaining a 3.0 GPA or better.

CHAPTER FOURTEEN

New Blood, New Glory—National Champions

Coach Stoops' first year marked the addition of new rules, new schemes, new blood, and new beginnings for OU. Rocky immediately loved Coach Brent Venables, his position coach. He was young, energetic, football-wise, listened to his players, and was very encouraging.

Torrance Marshall came to OU from Kemper Military; he and Rocky did not hit it off at first. Torrance wanted to run the show, but Rock said, "No." They pushed and shoved—and became friends. They learned and earned one another's respect. They both became defensive leaders. If number twenty didn't get you, number ten would. Because Rocky was a ranging guy, Coach Stoops shifted him to weak side linebacker, since, as Stoops said, "He's all over the field anyway."

Rocky's first game under Stoops was against Indiana State. Rocky took a nasty hit that bent his back awkwardly. The crowd moaned loudly, and Linda said it looked as though his back was about to break. But thank God, he returned to the game and just kept on going.

Rocky's game against Notre Dame was fun for the family—the legendary four horsemen, the heritage of the green and gold, and the heart-inspiring basilica of *Notre Dame* – despite the fact that OU lost. Rocky played against three of his old Jenks teammates – Andy Wisne, Shawn Mahan, and Jason Beckstrom. Rocky and fellow former-Trojan Cory Callens represented OU at this reunion. Rocky's high school friend, Sharon Watson, who was attending Notre Dame at the time, recommended that the family take time for sight-seeing, and they did not regret it!

Former Jenks Stars in the Notre Dame Game
Jason Beckstom, Shawn Mahan, Andy Wisne, Corey Callens, Rocky Calmus

That year's first game against Colorado was a big one for Rocky, since he tied the (Boz's) record of twenty-two tackles in one game – although the loss was a major disappointment to OU.

Coach Venables dubbed Rocky a "blue-collar player" with great ability, further mentioning that Rocky had a good attitude and had the ability "to fly" to the ball. Venables added that Rocky just had a "knack for finding the ball."

Rocky fractured his leg against Texas Tech and then rode home on a bus with his leg hanging down for seven or eight hours. However, he did play in the Bedlam game that year against OSU, and during the warm-ups, Rocky's adrenalin got pumping as he ran gently on his leg. And as Rocky got fired up, so did his teammates.

"Rocky secured our defense," said defensive coordinator Mike Stoops. "Just from a coaching standpoint, you like having those guys out there. He's very, very reliable, so it was a comforting thought to have him out there for Bedlam."

Though Rocky did not start, he came out during the third defensive series, amazing his teammates. Rodney Rideau said, "He's a tough cat; my hat is off to him. He's a great player and a tough guy."

"I could not cut as usual and was limited. I could have had twenty sacks on Lindsey [the OSU quarterback] if my leg had been good," Rocky said. Toward the third and fourth quarter, the pain started to bother Rocky, and he took himself out of the game. He had eight tackles and the respect of all the Sooner players, coaches, and fans.

Rocky's first college bowl game was against Mississippi, and though it was highly anticipated, it ended in a bitter loss—by only two points! It was hard to miss winning the Sandford Independence Bowl by such a small margin.

Some of Rocky's sophomore stats include being on the Associated Press All-Big XII team, being OU's MVP as the Defensive Player of the Year, and being on the Dallas Morning News' All-Big XII team. He led in quarterback hurries with eleven and was on the All Big XII first team.

Rocky's junior year, 2000, was unforgettable.. OU went 13-0, a perfect season. It was a perfect year except for a few injuries. But it was all worth a national championship. OU was the best in the Big XII and the best in the *nation*!

Rocky was listed as a pre-season All-American and one of the top five big hitters in the Big XII, and he did not let his team down.

Rocky said he was flattered by all the pre-season recognition but was quick to point out his sidekicks Torrance Marshall and Roger Steffam. They were voted as one of the nation's best units.

The "Boz" came back to OU several times, and Rocky could not believe that he called him by name. "How's it going, Rock?" Boz asked. He gave Rocky his phone number and told Rocky he'd lose it. Rock said he wouldn't—but he did. Rocky was sometimes compared to Boz, but the only thing they have in common is that they are both hard-hitting, tough linebackers.

Some of Rocky's faithful followers
Back L-R- John Baker, Tina Rowland, Mike Blue Cindy Musgrove, Kim McGehee, Samantha Blue
Middle- Myrle Calmus, Teri Marcum, Rocky, Linda Calmus, Radonn Musgrove
Front- Vicki Rowland, Althea Adams, Doris Vivian, Bilinda Baker

At the Red River Shootout, OU won 63-14—they were awesome, despite the wet, raining, nasty day. With his left arm in a long cast, fractured thumb extended, Rocky picked off a pass by Chris Sims and ran it forty-one yards for a touchdown. Fans and sports-lovers ran that clip over and over all year, and it was just as good every time. Quentin Griffin set a new OU school record with six touchdowns.

Rocky's lifelong supporters, the Musgroves, were sitting on the front row of a Texas game. Rocky spotted them and ran over, and that has also been replayed on various news clips often. Since his mother, Linda, and her sister, Cindy Musgrove, look so much alike, many people thought that Cindy was Rocky's mom—and thus Cindy became known as Rocky's "TV mom."

OU won against K-State amid a sea of rowdy purple cats. Linda's Kansas relatives were very supportive, wearing red in honor of Rocky. Linda was stunned and said that she wasn't sure she could have done that had their places been reversed. She remembered some of those games by saying, "Nebraska at Norman, pre-season national contenders, but the real Big Red stopped their hopes. OU 31, 14 November, Crouch didn't know what hit; it was the Sooner defense machine. Red October, beating Texas, K-State and Nebraska, how sweet it was when Norman was awakened by the Jolly Red Giant…beware!"

OU cruised through the Baylor Bears, 57-7, and Bob Stoops became a millionaire. Rocky felt he deserved it, however, and said, "He prepares every week. He works very hard, and the way he coaches equals wins."

That year's game against A&M was a nail-biter, and it looked bleak with the Aggies ahead. However, Torrance Marshall read the quarterback's eye and intercepted a pass. He ran thirty-two yards to the goal line, and Rocky helped keep him clear with two key blocks.

The Bedlam game that year was sloppy, and OU barely won, but Rocky helped clinch the win by getting a safety on Aso Poge. Linda almost didn't come because she and her grandson Tucker had the sniffles and it was a cold, damp day and the game was televised. Richie, said, "Mom, do you think Mrs. Heupel would miss a game?" Linda and Tucker felt guilty and got ready. Though she had to pay ninety dollars to sit in the east end zone and couldn't even see Rocky's safety, *but* she was there!

The Big XII Championship was against K-State—and yes, you can beat them twice. It was quite a game, and though it was cold, the game in Arrowhead Stadium was very memorable.

Rocky's awards for the season started rolling in. He was named Defensive Captain for the National Championship

Linda Calmus, Myrle Calmus, Clint Anderson, Teri Marcum, Mandy Calmus, Ashley Calmus, Richie Calmus, Lance Calmus, Skylar OBrien, Tucker Calmus, Rocky Calmus

squad, was the Associated Press' Big XII Defensive Player of the year, was the Defensive Player of the Week twice, and was one of three semi-finalists for the Butkus Award, then named the runner-up. He was also Consensus All-American and received the Walter Camp Award.

Rocky had 125 tackles, sixty-four of which were unassisted, and made seventeen tackles for loss. He had seven quarterback hurries, forced two fumbles, and had one interception for the run of forty-one yards and touchdown.

The Orange Bowl was an incredible experience for Rocky and the whole family. Over two-dozen family members and friends of the Calmus family went to Miami to see the game, and though the Florida State fans didn't give OU much of a chance, the team remained undeterred—they wanted a win. Linda said, "We're going to Miami, the Sooners in Miami! It's a dream from his freshman-losing season to a national championship contender—talk about emotions."

The usual crowd came—Pop and Mom Calmus, Rocky's brother Lance and his wife Ashley and son Tucker, Richie, Mandy, Aunt Cindy, Uncle John, cousins Kim McGehee and Preston, Dawn, John and wife Radonn and Blake and Thoren. In addition to family, friends Mike and Samantha Blue, neighbors Vicki and Tina Rowland and Doris Vivian also made the trip, as did friend and photographer Mary Engles and Rocky's former high school teammate, Dillon Engles. As well, the Bakers—John, Bilinda, Joseph, and Johnathan from Oklahoma City came. Rocky's girlfriend, Teri, and her brother Jake and father Steve also came. Rocky can't say he is not supported!

Tina Rowland put it this way: airfare, $400; lodging, $350; game tickets, $200; beating Florida State, **priceless**!

It was quite an extravaganza. Actor Denzel Washington performed the coin toss, Toby Keith sang the National Anthem, and famous people such as Tiger Woods and Alex Rodriguez watched from the sidelines.

Despite being the eleven-point underdogs going in, OU managed to beat Heisman Trophy winner Chris Weinke's Seminoles, nearly shutting them out. The evening climaxed as the fourth quarter ran down with the OU Sooners ahead of the FSU Seminoles 13-2, their only points from a safety from a botched kick that could have been worse without the kicker's fast reactions. Rocky sacked Weinke, causing a fumble and making for a high point of the entire game. He had six tackles and the fumble he created led to the only touchdown in the game—for OU. The young sophomores and juniors from OU gave quite a performance for the senior, seasoned Seminoles.

Celebrating after the Orange Bowl V ictory
Richie Calmus, Radonn Musgrove, Josh Heupel, John Musgrove, Mike Blue, and Rocky Calmus

The Sooners were the undisputed National Champions. The underdogs had stunned Florida State—along with the media and Lee Curso (who never gave OU a chance). Linda said, "Defense tossed another shutout—shocking, and just plain unbelief. The key, Sooner defense 13 & 0, opened the FSU lock-in; it doesn't get any better than this." Even Bobby Bowden said after the game that Miami probably deserved to play against the Sooners for the title—so much for the BCS ratings!

Rocky now had additional keepsakes to add to his high school championship rings, and he had the pride of knowing that he and his team had gone from the bottom to the top. What a ride! Rocky was grateful for the experience, and he credited the championship to the other players on the team, the excellent coaching staff, the die-hard fans, the university itself, and the trainers and doctors that helped make OU's victory possible.

CHAPTER FIFTEEN

Senior Year

As Rocky started his senior year at OU, his family was again fielding recruiters—though this time they're fighting over Rocky's pro career. Disappointingly, pre-season polls only ranked the National Champion Sooners as fourth in the nation. However, they were ranked number one in the Big XII South. Rocky was listed as one of the five heavy hitters in the nation. His handsome face graced the cover of six national magazines.

Rocky
Photo by Oklahoma University

Linda remembered that it was strange to go into a store and see her son's face on a magazine rack. She said she often wanted to shout, "See! That's my son!" but she resisted the urge.

Going into the season, Rocky said, "Everyone expects us to be good this year, and we are confident in ourselves." He went on to add, "We have a little strut in our walk—we're not cocky—but we definitely have a confident swagger. That's a given for any champion."

Many people rightly anticipated that Rocky would be the heart and soul of the defensive unit, a spiritual leader for the team. However, the Sooners had a bull's eye on their jerseys, and it was difficult to attempt a repeat. With Rocky, Teddy Lehman, and Jimmy Wilkerson, some thought OU might be even better than the year before—if that was possible.

One magazine took the time to discuss some of the things they were confident they wouldn't see, as well as those they were expecting, of Rocky that season. They went something like this:

Things you won't see: Oklahoma All-American linebacker Rocky Calmus walking into a meeting a tad late, sporting platinum-colored hair, wearing earrings or tattoos, or making headlines by getting DUI's, beating his girlfriend, or having a firearm.

Rocky making a blinding tackle

What you will see: Calmus making tackles, always being around the football, attending church, and giving 110 percent to his team and coaches.

To all appearances, Rocky is the "College Tough Man" that Sporting News has labeled him, but that is not the real Rocky. "I'm just a plain-Jane guy," Rocky said. "I love my girlfriend Teri, my dog Owen, [my] family, and especially my nephews, Tucker and Skylar." Even in his senior year, after having started the season as the MVP of the Hispanic Classic, Rocky was still his same old self. He has stayed true to his faith and his values, and he has not forgotten that his athletic ability is a gift from God.

OU continued to win, and Rocky usually had double-digit tackles. The first bump in that winning streak was against Nebraska. OU's trick play didn't work, but Nebraska's did! Even before they won, however, the Nebraska fans were very friendly.

OU had a shot at the Rose Bowl, but then a terrible upset occurred—in the Bedlam game OU's in-state rivals, OSU, who were 3-8, played their best game of their season. OSU won 16-13, dashing OU's national championship dreams for the year. OU had six scoring opportunities but no touchdowns to show for it. Sooner fans everywhere were stunned and sick at heart. There would be no trip to Pasadena, no BCS bowls.

It was a disappointing end to Rocky's last home game at OU, and it will always leave a bad taste in the mouths of OU fans everywhere. However, OU made it to the Cotton Bowl to play Arkansas and ended the season 10-2, which isn't a record of which fans should be ashamed. And OU *was* the National Championship team in 2000, and Rocky went away from that last regular season game knowing he had won numerous awards, made long-term friends, had played with great teammates and coaches, and had garnered a lot of media attention.

December 5, 2001 began the awards banquet tour. Rocky and family's first stop was for the Lombardi, a black-tie affair focused on four special young men, each of which deserved to be present. The event was held in Houston; Miss Texas was present, and Coach Capers (the new Houston NFL coach), was the keynote speaker. The finalists had the opportunity to visit a juvenile home and to spend some time with young cancer patients at one of the area's hospitals. The event raised $2.6 million that year.

Miss Texas, Stacy James, and Rocky at the Lombardi Awards

Each of the finalists received a beautiful wooden football with his name on it as well as numerous photographs to commemorate the occasion. The crowd went wild when they showed Rocky tackling Chris Sims in the UT game on the large video screen, but Julius Peppers ended up winning the award. Rocky also surprised a few people with his confident, friendly demeanor as he handled the little cancer patients, and Miss Texas actually commented on it. Rocky shows how much he loves children in how comfortable he is in picking up little ones; he loves his two nephews especially, and someday, years from now, he'll make a wonderful father.

Award number two was on ESPN and national TV, with Chris Fowler, Herbstreet, Curso, and Michelle. It was an exciting time, and there were so many awards!

Rock was also one out of three finalists for the Chuck Benarki (best defensive player) Award, but Peppers won again. Rocky was a member of the Walter Camp All-American Team. A lot of friends and family members were able to attend some of the later awards, including Teri and John and Radon Musgrove. Rock's longtime friend, Brett Butler, also got to help him celebrate.

John and Radonn were Disney club members and had a nice two-bedroom bungalow at Old Key West, so between awards ceremonies, the family went to Disney World, Pleasure Island, MGM, and Epcott Center.

The Bronco Nagurski was very nice, too, with over eight hundred people attending. Rocky's family did not receive a program or anything, though the sponsors would pay for his parents' meals and rooms. They didn't, however, pay for transportation to Charlotte, North Carolina, and because of the expense, there wasn't the usual entourage. The finalists all received a small, crystal OU football with their names engraved on them. Roy Williams from OU won, and everyone was very happy for him.

Rocky and best friend Brett Butler

OU's 2001 Award Program presented Rocky and Roy Williams with awards for being the Defensive Players of the Year, giving each one a pewter football with his stats on it.

Rocky's 2000 Butkus Award experience didn't go as planned. The awards were the real big time, with the thrills of ESPN, Disney World, the Hyatt-Grand Palace, and Hard Rock Live. Rocky's brothers and sister had to get to Florida at their own expense, and they only had one additional room provided for them; the girls stayed in that one, and the guys boarded with Rock in his room. They were large, beautiful—and expensive.

The first list of seventy of the top linebackers of the country was narrowed down to eleven and then later to three finalists, but the honor didn't go to Rock that year. It was probably the first time Rocky had lost something for which he had competed, but he was still honored. When asked how he really felt, he replied, "Honored to be one of the three best linebackers in the country—but yet disappointed." The family joke was that they went to the awards in a limousine but returned in a bus!

Butkus Awards 2000
Lance, Richie, Rocky, Dick Butkus, and Coach Tag Gross

The Butkus Award of 2001, however, was the most special event so far. The Butkus Award goes to the nation's top linebacker, and winning the award was one of Rocky's highest goals—he even named his dog Owen Butkus Calmus! The previous year, when Rocky was a runner-up, the event was a black-tie affair and was extremely elegant, but after the terrorist attack of September 11, the event lost its chief sponsor, Cooper Tires.

For a time it looked as though it was possible they were going to simply send the award to the winner.

Instead, the event was changed to a luncheon—no longer black-tie, but still very nice. At fifty dollars a guest, it was affordable, and there was even a contingent of OU fans in attendance who make their home in Florida—plus all the Calmus Clan.

Butkus Award 2001 Dick Butkus and Rocky
Photograph from the Orlando Sentinal

The best part of the event wasn't the food, the support, or the posh amenities—the highlight of the evening was when they called **Rocky Calmus' name as the winner of the 2001 Butkus Award!** Dick Butkus presented the trophy to Rock, saying, "This is an individual award given because the young man earns it. It is not [based] on his draft potential or his future career path but just [on his] hard work and skill as a college player."

The Calmuses were of course incredibly proud of Rocky, and they were also very thankful to those involved in making them feel so welcome even before Rocky won the award. Shelly Ferguson, the executive director, was a very organized, efficient, and beautiful woman; she made everything run smoothly.

Stewart Hill, who provided transportation for the Calmuses, was an accommodating young man that they all enjoyed very much. The president of the Athletic Club, Don Landry, and the chairman, Chip Landon, were spectacular hosts and went out of their way to make everyone feel comfortable. It was very special to have OU's Head Coach, Bob Stoops, as well as, both Co-defensive Coaches, Mike Stoops and Brent Venables present. OU Sport's Director, Kenny Mossaman attended, too.

Rocky's trophy case holding the Butkus Award

The trophy itself was awesome; it is twenty inches tall, weighs thirty-five pounds, and depicts a linebacker with golden arms and legs, a dark blue number fifty-one jersey, and a gold helmet with a cutout face mask. It was a little difficult carrying it home on the plane, but Rocky's dad, Myrle, cradled it like his prized possession. Rocky cherishes it above all the other awards he has won thus far.

Mryle and Linda Calmus
at the Butkus Awards

The Calmus Family at the Butkus Awards
Lance, Mandy, Rocky, Linda, Myrle, and Richie

CHAPTER SIXTEEN

Picking Cotton, Not Roses

If only we had a little more offense. If only our trick play worked against Nebraska. If only we had not been beaten at Bedlam (OSU game) by a field goal. If only . . .

The defense carried OU but it was not enough. Yeah, 11-2, and that is still a great record. So to big "D" (Dallas) we go to play our bordering neighbors of Arkansas. Those "hogs" came out in full force, but the Sooner "nation" did too. It was a morning game at 10 A.M.—cold, damp, and everyone not quite awake, but it did not last long. The whistle blew and it was business as usual. It was an exciting game, defensive in nature. All the boys looked like green men from another planet, the grass painted green showing easily on those white uniforms.

Family friend and photographer, Mary Engles

With my press credentials secured, camera, wide-angle zoom lens, and unipod in tow, I made my way past the crowds, down the tunnel, and onto the football field. OU players ran out onto the field, and as had been his tradition, Rocky was the last player out. The defense, with Rocky and Roy Williams as leaders, played a tough game. Thousands watched the game from the stands and on television, but not many could follow Rocky right after the game. I'm proud of Rocky and was impressed and excited to be allowed to do so right after the 2002 SBC Cotton Bowl.

Immediately following the final play, I found Rocky on the football field; television cameras and reporters, each wanting an interview, surrounded the proud Butkus winner. He stood right next to Bob Stoops as the winning trophy was presented. Exhausted but still exhilarated, Rocky headed to the locker room—not to shower and rest but to celebrate for a few moments with the team—and then he quickly was escorted to the press building for interviews with ESPN. I was waiting with the press in a large building. The room sat fifty people, all waiting to ask questions of the players and coaches. The back portion of the room was filled with twenty to thirty TV cameras standing neatly in two rows on tripods on risers so that all the cameras got a clear shot.

Quinton Griffin entered the room first, followed by Rocky, Bob Stoops, Frank Romero, and then Trent Smith. Though the interviews were televised, I don't think you could see Rocky's proud smile as he watched Quinton (who was a bit timid about public speaking) get up and take questions as the Offensive Player of the Game.

Rocky, along with Coach Stoops and the other players, answered questions and then were escorted to another room for individual press interviews. I followed Rock through the curtain and was attempting to head to the next room when a security officer informed me that I was not to go beyond that point. Rocky was walking ahead of me, being interviewed, but he turned and said, "She's with me." Those were the magic words I needed to continue.

I followed Rocky as one reporter handed him a cell phone by which he was being interviewed by ESPN live. He paused from the interview to say, "Mary, do you have your cell phone? Please call my mom. I don't want her to wait out in the cold too long. Tell my family to head back to the hotel to wait for me, because I'm going to be a while." I was wondering what I would do for a ride without them, but Rocky continued, saying, "You stay right with me and we'll ride back on the bus."

"She's with me" Rocky and Mary Engles
Photo by Jimmy Busellato

I thought, here he is with a national sports media interviewing him, and he's more concerned about his family. I called Linda, his mom, and told her I wished she could see her son as he calmly and intelligently answered all the questions coming at him from various members of the news media. The TV cameras right in his face did not seem to faze him, and he seemed a nat ural in front of the spotlight.

He had green paint from the field all over his uniform and even on his face, dried blood caked on his leg where a large patch of skin was scraped during a play, and he was tired and hungry. Did he complain or stop the interviews? No, not Rocky.

I later asked him his thoughts when he was sitting on that podium with the press pounding one question after another. He said, "I almost fell asleep I was so tired." He could have fooled me! He was so articulate and clear with each answer.

Security finally did put a stop to the interviews and escorted Rocky and me—he again told them, "She's with me; make sure she gets in the van"—outside to a waiting van. Rock signed autographs along the way.

They took us back to the locker room for Rock to finally get that hot shower, but first I was able to take a picture of Rocky next to his locker at the Cotton Bowl before we were quickly escorted outside. He scrubbed in vain trying to remove that green field paint from his nose! I was taken into the locker room but placed in a side room until the boys were presentable.

The buses with players and coaches had long since left and headed back to the hotel, but two police cars were waiting outside the locker room. Security escorted Rocky to the open car door, but he would not get in. He asked, "Where's Mary? Don't leave her behind, she's with me." When I got in, the police car sped off with Rocky, Trent Smith, and me back to the hotel where family and friends were waiting.

Rocky is always so good with young, adoring fans—he paused for autographs and pictures with seven excited boys, all clad in OU number twenty jerseys with their faces painted crimson and red, when we reached the hotel. After more autographs, we got into the elevator and headed to his hotel room where Rocky could finally rest. However, with many family and friends waiting, Rock was again the courteous one, signing more autographs, smiling for pictures, and thanking individuals for coming to watch him play. Coaches Bob Stoops and Brent Venables came to congratulate Rocky and other players and pause for more pictures.

I even had my picture taken with Rocky; I asked him to sign my number twenty jersey and SBC Cotton Bowl media guide, and he was glad to oblige, for "she's with me."

Thanks, Rocky!

Rocky's pride and joy
Nephews, Skylar O'Brien, and Tucker Calmus

Coach Bob Stoops and Rocky

Nephew, Tucker Calmus and Rocky
Tucker waited in line with everyone else to get Rocky's autograph

CHAPTER SEVENTEEN

The Senior Bowl and the First Look at the NFL

Linda Calmus

The calls have begun in earnest again—agents, attorneys, and financial advisors. How do you pick? We've spent a lot of time praying, interviewing, and talking with OU coaches and the parents of various NFL players. One parent warned us that Rocky would soon be considered a "piece of meat," since he'll be on the block at the Senior Bowl.

The Senior Bowl is very important. Taking place in Mobile, Alabama, it is by *invitation* only, and it is the bowl game that gives students the publicity they need to make a good impression and get recruited; it is a gathering of the best college players in the nation. It is also the first time that NFL coaches and managers get to see the student athletes up close and personally. They will observe the potential recruits' work ethics, their abilities, skills, weaknesses, and adaptability.

The teams in the Senior Bowl each had roughly six linebackers per team, and each of these players played about half the game. Rocky had a good showing, making ten tackles—not too shabby! The commentators harped on his small size, but he made the big plays, "small" size and all. The South won, but it wasn't really much of a contest.

The Calmus family had fun, and they stayed busy by meeting with various agents. It turned out to be a difficult decision, because they were all nice, knowledgeable, and full of promises. Rocky chose a man that wasn't too flashy—a good, Christian family man with whom Rock felt comfortable—and had a compatible personality. Mark, Rocky's new agent, was ready for him to travel to Phoenix, Arizona, to view the workout facility and increase his strength, weight, and speed. Rocky loved the facility and began diligently preparing for the Combine, an opportunity for young athletes to showcase their skills.

Rocky reported that eating six times a day really wasn't as much fun as it sounded; he works out regularly with Mia Hamm and Ricky Williams. "It's a science," he said. You "lift, pump up, eat, and get bigger. I would really like to continue to do this, if I can afford it; this makes a difference."

Rocky Calmus—The Combine: February 28, 2002–March 4, 2002

How will I test? Will I be stronger with more weight on my frame? Will I be faster? Only time will tell. I am asked which team I would prefer to be drafted by all the time, but I usually answer that I just want the opportunity to play. I have always liked Dallas, but they have pushed me to the edge; and it would be nice to be close to Oklahoma so my parents, family, and friends can attend games.

I want to thank my family—my parents, brothers, sister, sister-in-law, nephews, aunts, uncles, cousins, and grandmothers—as well as my friends and faithful neighbors for all the support they've given me over the years. They've all spent a lot of time and money traveling to my games, and I truly appreciate it. I'm thankful for all my OU brothers, especially Roy Williams who talks about the devotion of my family as they stand "thirty-deep."

Rocky
Photo by Jana Monlapig

Football is a game I love and a challenge I embrace, and I hope it will be the same at the next level. Sure, right now it is all business, but I still have to have fun! I want to thank the Lord once more for the talent and perseverance He has given me. I've been truly blessed, and I thank Him for enabling me to do all things by the strength He's given me, as it says in Philippians 4:13.

Linda Calmus

I want to say that it has been phenomenal; thanks, OU, for giving us so many memories! There are so many unsung heroes from the ticket office to the academic office to the sports information department—teachers, trainers, coaches, doctors, and fans—that we probably never will get to thank properly. Rocky has been so very blessed!

Thank you, Rock, for all your hard work in the classroom as well as on the field. Your dad and I have been told over and over again what a good role model you are, how children look up to you, and how many people have enjoyed your career.

With tears streaming down my face, there is not much more to be said. Thank you, Rocky! Thank you, Lord! We will be waiting for the next level—the NFL. Continue to be "Rock Solid" and you can't lose!

Linda and Myrle Calmus

CHAPTER EIGHTEEN

You've Got Rock Questions, We've Got Answers

Rocky's mother Linda recorded his answers to some of the more common questions fans ask of him, and most of these have been included here, though he chose not to answer some.

Nickname or names, and how did you get them?

I suppose my most common nickname is "the Rock." I remember my senior year in high school, my family decorated my pickup truck. Uncle Richard and Dad made a huge rock out of papier-mâché and chicken wire. My artist uncle painted it, and it really looked like a huge rock. Everyone was amazed—it was unusual, since no one else had a rock on his truck.

Other names:

Rocky Steady, Rocky Top, Rocko, Rockster, Rockles, and, of course, Rock Solid.

Who is your all-time favorite OU player?

Spencer Tillman would have to be my all-time favorite. When I was a kid, he spoke at my brother Richie's fifth grade football banquet, and I've liked him ever since that. Richie took his number twenty, and I have continued it. I really wanted number eight or nine in college, but they were taken, and all of my family members had number twenty items. Although it is not a linebacker number, it has been good for me.

Of course, the Boz is also a favorite of mine. He is way cool. Tony Casillis is also great, and Steve Owens…there are so many!

Have you missed playing offense?

I do miss running a lot; everybody wants to be an offensive player for some reason. Fans like to see the big plays, and I miss helping the team score. My first love in football was running the ball. I've done that since the third grade.

How do you calm yourself down before a game?

I don't get overly excited, because you can't be too high or too low. You have to find a happy medium. Ninety percent of the game is played from the neck up.

What is your take on your studies, football, and all you have to do?

My job as a scholar athlete is first to schoolwork, then to football. First of all, you have to get your academics so you will be eligible. School, practice, study, and sleep—that's about it.

Your first year at OU, you lost more times than your entire grade school and high school years; what were your thoughts on that?

That was tough to swallow, having that many losses, because I'd never had a losing season. [From third grade through twelfth grade, he only had lost three games.] I didn't know what to think when the new head Coach, Bob Stoops, arrived at OU. But after seeing him assemble his staff, I was more optimistic about the future of OU football.

Your interviews are so well done; do you have hints on how you handle the media?

Over time, having to answer so many rapid-fire questions, you just get used to it.

Do you have any pre-game traditions?

No, not really. I'm always the last man out of the tunnel, but that just kind of evolved. I listen to music before games; all kinds of music—country, rap, etc.

Why do you not walk out with the captains?

Because I'm the last man out; I'm not being arrogant, it's just my ritual.

Were you the first OU player to start going to the fans after a game for high fives and congratulations?

No, the team just kind of made it happen.

Are you superstitious?

No.

Have you ever been scared that if you got hurt or if you didn't make it to the pros that you would be letting a lot of people down?

Lots of people have expectations, but I would not feel I was letting them down. I put more pressure on myself than anyone else puts on me.

What NFL team has been your favorite?

As a child, my favorite team was Dallas. Now? Dallas, but they are pushing me to the edge!

Do you think an 8.5 to 9 degree driver would make you hit the golf ball down the middle of the fairway?

I don't know what would help me drive it down the fairway!

How have you stayed with one girlfriend for so long?

She's a beautiful young lady that I enjoy spending time with; it's not that hard.

What is your favorite movie?

I really don't have one because I'm too busy with studies, practice, and football games to go to movies.

Advice to young want-to-be's?

To you future young athletes: All things are possible. Chase your dreams! I'm not the biggest or the fastest linebacker. Size doesn't matter; you have to put your heart into it, and set your mind to it. I hope I'm a pretty good example of that. Remember Philippians 4:13!

Thanks for the memories!

Coach Roger Dicus, Rocky, Dillon Engles,
Coach Jim Butler, Brett Butler, Todd Rosenthal

5th grade
Rocky and Dillon Engles

Jenks High School- #20 Rocky, #2 Brett Butler, #1 John Johnston, #70 Jason Lohr

Left to Right: Uncle Gene, Aunt Jessie Longhofer, Uncle John Musgrove
Linda, sister Cindy Musgrove, and Myrle

Lance and Ashley Calmus

Rocky and Ryan Fisher

Cousin Derek, Aunt Paula, Rocky, Uncle Gary,
Richie Calmus, Sandra, and Max Ridgeway

Preston McGehee, Rice Owl Mascot, Kim McGehee

Grandma Pauline Calmus
and Uncle Richard Calmus

Back- Samantha Blue, Cousin Dawn, John Baker,
Rocky, Aunt Cindy, Bilinda Baker,
Front- Mike Blue, Sydney Blue, Joseph Baker, April

Rocky and Teri Marcum

Neighbors
Tina Rowland, Doris Vivian, and Vicki Rowland

Rocky taking care of business
Photo by Mark Kraus

Josh Heupel and Rocky

Rocky and OU Teammates
#89 Cory Heinecke, #20 Rocky, and #11 Teddy Lehman

R
O
C
K
Y

Rocky's touchdown at Texas
Picked up by friend and former Jenks teammate, Cory Callens

2001 Red River Shootout
Photo by University of Oklahoma

Photo by Jana Monlapig

Photo by Jana Monlapig

Photo by Jimmy Busellato

Linda Calmus and Julie Luke
Photo by Jimmy Busellato

Accomplishments

High School

Rocky was named:

- All-Conference
- All-State
- All-American
- Jim Thorpe/Daily Oklahoman "Defensive Player of the Year"
- Carrier 388 tackles, 2823 yards rushing, and 49 touchdowns

Rocky played both linebacker and running back in high school . . . A three year starter who helped his squad to a combined 39-2 overall record.

College
Freshmen 1998-1999

- One of the top freshmen in the Big 12 Conference
- Earned second team freshmen All-American honors from the *Sporting News*
- Finished the year fifth on his squad with 55 tackles, including 30 unassisted . . . Total of eleven tackles for loss, was the third best total on the squad and the sixteenth best in the Big 12
- Played in all eleven games as a member of the special teams and defensive unit.
- First Career start in OU's game at Missouri . . . Finished that contest with eight tackles, a blocked extra point, and blocked punt
- Averaged 7.8 tackles a game as a starter
- Awarded in 1998 The University of Oklahoma Special Team Player of the Year

Sophomore 1999-2000

- 1999 labeled by Sooner coaches as the top defensive player on the squad
- Earned first team All-Big 12 honors from *The Dallas Morning News*
- Led the team in 114 tackles, including a team-best 76 unassisted
- Had six games with 10 or more tackles
- Tied the school record for tackles in a game by a linebacker (set by Brian Bosworth in 1986 against Miami) with 22 tackles against Colorado
- Had double-digit tackle games against Indiana State (11), Louisville (10), Texas (13), Missouri (11) and Iowa State (10)
- Led the squad in quarterback hurries with 11
- Academic All-Big 12 first team
- Big 12 Conference Jan Myers (Outstanding Freshmen Award for Excellence in Academics and Athletics)
- Oklahoma Football OU 1st team
- Academic All Big 12
- Chevrolet MVP of the OU vs Colorado for outstanding performance (22 tackles)

Junior 2000-2001

- Finalist for the Butkus Award as one of the nations best linebackers
- Named first-team concensus All-American by the Football Writers Association and the Walter Camp Foundation
- Leads the team in tackles with 125 total, including 64 unassisted
- Has recorder 10 or more tackles four times this season
- Had a pair of 17-tackle performances against Nebraska and Texas A&M
- Played almost the entire season with a broken bone just above his right thumb
- Chosen by teammates as a Team Captain
- Chevrolet Scholarship Program 2000 Chevrolet Division I "Defensive Player of the Year" University of Oklahoma
- University of Oklahoma Linebacker Rocky Calmus has been named the **Toughest College Football Player** in the nation by *The Sporting News*
- Rocky Calmus In Appreciation for the Christian example you set for others to follow NYI, Tulsa Southwest Nazarene Church February 28, 2001

Senior 2001-2002

- Chosen by teammates as Team Captain
- First Team All-American concensus(FWAA, Walter Camp, AFCA, The Sporting News, CNNSI.com)
- Second Team All-American (Football News)
- First Team All-Big 12 (AP, Big 12 Coaches, Football News, Dallas Morning News, College Football News.com)
- Lombardi Award Finalist
- Bednarik Award Finalist
- Butkus Award Winner
- OU vs N.C. 2nd Annual Hispanic College Fund Football Classic, Most Valuable Player, Big 12 All-Academic
- 2001 Oklahoma Football Defensive Most Valuable Player:
- School Record-Career tackles for loss-57
- School Record-Career tackles for loss by a linebacker-57
- School Record-Starts by a linebacker-41